PRAISE F̵[barcode]

THE INTENTIONAL ENTREPRENEUR

"*The Intentional Entrepreneur* gives you everything you need to ensure your brand is working 24 hours a day to meet your goals and realize your dreams. I keep five books within arm's reach at all times and this is one of them."

David Conley / Serial Entrepreneur

"It is easy to underestimate or deny the impact of one's personal brand. But with the increasing pervasiveness of social media, online communities, and digital commerce, executives can no longer choose *not* to have a public persona. Today, the choice is whether you will intentionally shape your personal brand so that it expresses your priorities and values, or instead allow your reputation to be randomly defined by external forces. Jen Dalton's new book takes you through a simple yet comprehensive process for exploring what your image is now, deciding what message you want your image to convey, and intentionally building a reputation that delivers value for you and your business. The book is easy to read, filled with great wisdom and insights, and jammed with exercises that will help enable you to apply that wisdom to your own situation. Whether you are a fledgling entrepreneur who is just starting a business or a seasoned CEO trying to navigate our changing digital world, this book will help you to better shape your own reputation and project a public image that works to further your, and your company's, success."

Bill Yoder / Senior Associate, Springboard International Inc.

"Jen Dalton has crafted a timely and relevant guide on how entrepreneurs should navigate the challenging waters of defining your image. In an environment where social media plays an ever-increasing role in defining your personal brand, Ms. Dalton leverages real-world examples to illustrate how she has helped businesses enact transformative changes. The inclusion of key tools, and enabling the reader to take the same steps forward in defining his or her own personal brand all make it a must read for any aspiring entrepreneur!"

Michael Cheung / Vice President, Fast Pay

"As most lawyers know, you cannot go too far in private practice without an entrepreneurial drive. This book is essential for all junior and mid-career lawyers who are developing their practice. Ms. Dalton's book provides clear and direct guidance for professionals to enhance their personal brand with short checklists and exercises. Whether you need to refine your "elevator pitch" or identify what sets you apart from your competition (your value proposition), the short chapters will guide you through the process. The text expands beyond the basics to help the professional understand and communicate the differentiation and synergies between their brand and their company's brand, as well as enhancing the reader's understanding of networking techniques (in-person and via social media), the importance of personal presentation, and market segment prioritization and expansion."

Law Firm Executive

"Jen Dalton has created an easy to read and easy to adopt approach to evaluating one's self and its intertwined relationship with your business goals. The step by step approach is thought-provoking to those just starting and presents gentle reminders for those more seasoned folks on the Entrepreneurial journey."

Becca Rosner / Founder, Zophy Studios

"This book is a well-written, thoughtful and concise blueprint for how to successfully leverage your own and your company's brand. It is a practical guide that offers insights into how to think about key elements of your business, and offers a platform for success. The book goes beyond just the usual pronouncements, offering entrepreneurs a step-by-step approach to thinking about what makes them and their businesses different, and what their value proposition really is. A must read for any business leader. An indispensable guide to successful entrepreneurship."

Raad Alkadiri / Managing Director, HIS

"I just finished Jen Dalton's new book, *The Intentional Entrepreneur*, which outlines how new and current entrepreneurs can build their personal brand as they build their business. It's fantastic. Even if you aren't starting a new enterprise, there are strong insights into building your message and brand that are relevant—no matter your current role."

Jessica Salmoiraghi / Director, Federal Agencies and International Programs, American Council of Engineering Companies

"Ms. Dalton hits on a blind spot for many entrepreneurs who are understandably so pre-occupied with the "what" and "how" of building their company that they forget to focus on the "who" that is so critical for connecting to the hearts of their customers—where all valuable relationships begin. The great CEOs all have bigger-than-life reputations, but she shows that developing the proper persona is a process—one that all entrepreneurs can learn. It's not luck or innate talent, but being a "noisebreaker" instead of just another noisemaker is as simple as having intention and walking through a series of tools that Ms. Dalton presents throughout this book."

Rob Cimperman / President, Cimperman, LLC.

"Amazing, content rich and packed with a tremendous amount of insights, ideas, and tools to take control over your personal brand and share you value to the world. Great job, Jen!"

John Harrison / CEO, Cybexa

"The book was very easy to read and I appreciated the real world examples. You don't have to be a CEO or own your own company to get tremendous value from reading this book."

Sara Mastro / Senior Director, Media Barn, Inc.

"Jen Dalton's first book, *The Intentional Entrepreneur*, offers a useful guide for building a CEO's digital reputation and integrating it into their company's brand. She combines step by step processes with interesting examples from friends, clients, and famous entrepreneurs. Despite its focus on entrepreneurs, the lessons are applicable to anyone who values the importance of building their brand and reputation through the variety of digital tools available. Although you might not be a CEO, you still want to develop a unique brand that complements that of your current company while positioning you for future opportunities. A quick initial read, *The Intentional Entrepreneur* offers a lot of ideas to consider and resources to utilize while planning a visibility strategy, creating a company, or planning to take a company to the next step. So important to be a "Noisebreaker", as Jen suggests, cutting through the noise and adding value to your audience to build your brand!"

Emily Muth / Consultant, Excella Consulting

"The Intentional Entrepreneur serves multiple purposes for the rising or seasoned real estate entrepreneur! With its' step-by-step tools following on very helpful explanations of how to create one's business, the book can be very useful to companies who have post-licensing training for new agents to create their business. The processes delineated in each chapter serve to highlight the steps many real estate companies try to "teach" their self-employed agents and it will serve as a useful tool to seasoned agents who are "mentoring" newbies. The first chapters on defining who you are and your brand are especially useful in this endeavor. The later chapters serve to "spark" seasoned agents who need rejuvenation—should they start a "team" or move out on one's own to create one's own Brokerage. Ms. Dalton has given much to think about and a process to help one create the next important steps. The book is a wonderful blend of provoking important "thought" to "couch" one's business and then the tools to become successful. Clearly, the focus on social media is key in this age when Realtors are challenged from all directions from "others" wanting to get into their business. Ms. Dalton has provided a wonderful book and tool for anyone wanting to be a successful Realtor."

Nancy Kane / ABR, SRES, AHS, Associate Broker, Weichert Realtors

Have you ever thought of building something great? What's the first step in making that happen? The Intentional Entrepreneur puts framework around your idea. Whether you are beginning your journey or want to further develop your brand, this book offers something for every business creator. Thoughtfully laid out, Jen takes you on the path to branding something unique and intentional. With so many brands to choose from, The Intentional Entrepreneur will most definitely show you how to be a noisebreaker, not a noisemaker.

Tina Fox / CEO, Tina Fox Consulting

"I wish that I was able to have this information and content when I started my business. Jen Dalton captures the entrepreneur's mindset and knows what it is needed to think things through when having a start-up, which ultimately leads to better cost-savings, strategy and focus. I highly recommend this book!"

Laura Lee Williams / CEO & Founder, Laura Lee Designs, Inc.

As a Montessori teacher setting out to develop my own brand of an alternative gifted and talented program (GETS -Gifted Education Time for Students), I GET the value of this book! The path is clear and I am free to follow it at MY OWN PACE within the carefully planted guideposts set out by Jen Dalton (I find the www.brandmirror.com imbedded links very handy). Her worksheets are sequentially planned, making them particularly useful in creating a solid base upon which to construct my business. Concentrating information in an easy to access place also saves me time and money, allowing me to allocate scarce funds at appropriate times. It is a brave and gutsy thing to lay your dream before strangers and ask them to believe in it as deeply as you do yourself. Following Jen Dalton's advice makes that task less of a "risk and judgement" based exercise and more of a relaxing procedure. Procedures are neither good nor bad...just stages to pass through on your way to completing a task. Ms. Dalton's chapters are peppered with real life examples and referral names to help me attend to particulars when I am ready, such as tax and legal advice, trademarking, and the ever present social media "pit of despair". Ms. Dalton explains clearly that social media is a tamable beast and again, there are procedures and real life examples to inform my choices of when, where and how to engage. Creating MY BRAND and infusing it with meaning that will permeate MY community, small or large-is work that I must do for myself, but Ms. Dalton's advice allows me to re-charge my energy and move forward...always forward toward my goal.

Dolores Peck / My Academic Coach founder and creator of the GETS Hands On Humanities Program.

Noisebreakers — Intentional Entrepreneur expands your thinking beyond who or what you think your business is. It makes you take a step back and see your business as yourself so that you can stand out from the noise and be the brand in demand you are meant to be.

Sherrell T. Martin / CEO, Nitram Financial www.nitramfinancial.com

"A great and informative read, wherever the journey of entrepreneurship finds you. There are sections for the beginner and the seasoned adventurer; there's real substance here for everyone. Jen Dalton sheds light in a way that is informative and accessible; I love her written voice. Enjoy, and learn something new!"

Michael Sauri / President & Co-Owner, TriVistaUSA

THE **INTENTIONAL ENTREPRENEUR**

How to Be a Noisebreaker, Not a Noisemaker

BY JEN DALTON

COPYRIGHT

DISCLAIMER

Cover Design: John Matthews

Interior Design: Heidi Miller

Editing: Mila Nedeljkov

Author's photo courtesy of Jason Pentecost

DEDICATION

To my family, thank you for being on this journey with me: Jerrod, Wyatt, Logan, Carol, and David. You inspire me to be my best self.

TABLE OF CONTENTS

FOREWORD

You cannot <u>not</u> communicate. Debated by communication scholars for years, this idea has never been more relevant than in today's mediated environment. We have access to more channels than ever before to connect with our audiences. As norms around user expertise and facility with social media have evolved, expectations for conversing with leaders online are growing.

Many executives believe that their business is not conducive to social media, or that their customers are not on social media, and convince themselves that they don't have to develop a presence within the online environment. However, each time a potential new customer or stakeholder searches for those executives in LinkedIn, Facebook, Instagram, or any number of social media spaces and comes up with nothing, those executives are communicating a message. By not being in those spaces, stakeholders may believe executives do not value their voice, are not relevant, or even worse, have nothing of value to contribute to the conversation.

No online presence conveys a message just as creating a presence online does. Jennifer Dalton, in her book, *The Intentional Entrepreneur*, helps executives weigh the choices associated with building a reputation for business online.

Which platforms should be considered? Where to develop expertise and contribute to the dialogue? Where should that dialogue take place?

I am an Associate Professor at Georgetown University in the Communication, Culture and Technology Program with an affiliate appointment in the McDonough School of Business. Over the past twenty years I have researched and taught about the impact of communication technologies on developing and managing our presence. I met Jennifer when I taught her Management Communication course in the Executive MBA program. Jennifer and I clicked immediately because of her dedication to understanding the development of executive presence, and her interest in the burgeoning platforms offered by online environments.

In spring of 2014, I invited Jennifer to work with me on a seminar for graduate students that helped them explore their personal narratives and create digital portfolios for articulating that narrative to their key external audiences. She has built on many of the ideas that she developed in that course to create a clear, step-by-step approach for identifying and positioning key strengths.

Jennifer has worked with dozens of executives and uses case studies from her experience to provide a comprehensive three-pronged approach:

1. Real examples of everyday business owners discovering their WHY

2. Showcasing what they can and should talk about to augment the business strategy, and considering where this conversation should take place

3. Leveraging their reputation to make an impact in intentional and authentic ways

It is true that you don't have to participate in every online environment. You don't have time to do that. However, you can't ignore the need to have an online presence. If you do, you are sending a message that your voice and expertise are not relevant to a huge group of stakeholders. I encourage you to take the time to work through these chapters and use the tools to identify the platforms that make sense for you, the shareholders that matter to you, and the expertise you would like to cultivate. Be thoughtful and intentional about how you manage your presence. If you are not strategically thinking through these questions, someone else will be attributing ideas to you based on your absence in the conversation.

Congratulations for taking the first step in addressing your brand presence. Developing these themes will help in the construction of your online conversations and expertise as well as support the foundation that you have already created offline. Follow Jen's path, and intentionally join the conversation.

Jeanine Warisse Turner, PhD / Associate Professor, Georgetown University | Executive MBA Program | Communication, Culture, Technology Program

INTRODUCTION

How this book helps YOU: the Founder & CEO

> "If people like you they will listen to you, but if they trust you, they'll do business with you."
>
> **ZIG ZIGLAR**

You are getting ready to start on a very personal and very intentional journey, launching a company and leading it so that it reflects your purpose and values, while making a difference to those you serve. The most critical element as a CEO and leader is that people trust you and want to work with you. Your reputation precedes you, so how are you managing those perceptions?

This book is your guide through this process. You will learn why trust matters and how to build it with people in an intentional and powerful way. Each chapter will guide you through the personal branding process and help you understand how it relates to your business and why. It will help you tell your story in a way that helps you stand out and build the best relationships to grow your business with clarity and meaning.

This book is for you if:

- You are looking for a clear, actionable process that provides tangible steps on building a reputation that drives growth, visibility, and impact for you and your business

- You hunger for specific examples of entrepreneurs leveraging their personal brand from the launch of their business (deciding what to name the business and ensuring it resonated with them personally)

- You are launching a new business and need to figure out how best to use online tools to grow visibility — like LinkedIn, Hootsuite, and new channels like Blab

- You want to build a company that is grounded in your values and the vision you have for making a meaningful difference in the world

This book is your guide through this process of **intentionally** discovering, validating, and building a reputation that delivers value for you and your business. Each chapter will enable you to be more authentic, generate trust, and create relevance through your reputation as the CEO.

This book will help you understand:

- How personal branding relates to your business and why

- How you are unique and why people should do business with you

- What questions to ask when figuring out how to blend your personal reputation and brand with the company brand over time

- How to create a visibility plan that builds the best relationships to grow your business with clarity and meaning

- Identify practical ways to manage your online reputation and presence for your brand as the CEO, given you only have so much time in the day

Let's face it — in the beginning it is your reputation that IS the business, your ability to connect with people and help them understand how committed you are and what is it exactly about you that can help them. It is hard to sit down and come up with words to describe yourself; it is a type of soul-searching which can be as painful as writing a resume, or even just talking about what you do. The steps and insights in this book provide clarity on how to talk about yourself and market your skills so you stand out in a confident and approachable way.

Developing an Authentic and Compelling Reputation is Key

When you start your business, it is important to be consistent, clear, and compelling around what is unique about you and your company. Persuading people to change their habits or try something new is very challenging, so connecting with them in a way that resonates with them is essential.

Your business is a reflection of you: it exhibits your values, your ideas, and your goals for this point in your life and years to come. Developing your business from the beginning with you, your customers, and your goals in mind is the key to success and near-term and sustained growth.

People make decisions based on a first impression in less than 10 seconds; in this book you will learn how to deliver an outstanding first impression. Then, once you are in the door, the buying process can be even more challenging, depending on your business and also on you. This book provides actionable insights to get you in the door, which is part of the buying process, and how to do it authentically. As you learn about your potential clients and talk through solutions with them, it is critical that your messaging is well defined and resonates with your potential clients. The more clarity you have on your reputation and what it means to work with you, the easier it will be for people to trust you and want to work with you.

Your personal brand is who you are, it is what you represent, and most importantly it is what makes you unique. You may think that anyone can do what you do, or have concerns about how to be different. By the end of this book you will know why you are different, how to help others see that, and how to be so darn interesting that people will want to do business with you any day of the week.

Remember the dentist targeted for killing Cecil the Lion? His personal decision to go on that hunt and then post pictures crushed his reputation, his family, and his business for several months. There are stories from small business owners to big business CEOs that have been hung by the digital jury for crimes that may (or may not) have been fitting of the punishment. Either way, your personal life is blended in many ways with your professional life, for better or worse.

People are defining your reputation every day, don't you want to be in charge of that? It is no longer an option to opt out of reputation management, especially as a CEO. The good news is that the internet is here, and anyone can make a difference and have a voice; the bad news is that the internet is here, and the bar is set higher when it comes to managing your online reputation as a CEO and as the face of the company. If you want to see how you are doing, take this personal brand assessment and see how you score.

For Your Eyes Only

We have made these worksheets available on our website too, along with other bonus material. You can visit www.brand mirror.com, look on the Book drop down titled "Worksheets and Tools", visit to access three resources for you. Simply enter "noisebreaker" to access the following: The Intentional Entrepreneur Workbook (or you can write in the book), Bonus Chapter on LinkedIn for Business, and Tools, a short document that lists all the tools we discuss here. We will update the materials on a regular basis. If you are on our email list, we will let you know when we make changes.

Reputation Assessment for Entrepreneurs

(A=Awesome, C=Close to Done, F=Focus Needed, Z=Asleep, Not Done) A=10, C=5, F=1, Z=0

Understand Your Current Reputation & Where You Want to Go		Points
Discover & Know Yourself	☐ You have mapped the key moments that shaped you	_____
	☐ You have identified your top 5 values.	_____
	☐ You have identified your top 5 strengths.	_____
Define Your Reputation	☐ You have identified the top words associated with your brand	_____
	☐ You have outlined your leadership promise statement.	_____
	☐ You have identified gaps in perception & reality	_____
Differentiate Yourself	☐ You have identified competitors and how your voice / reputation is unique.	_____
	☐ You have developed your unique knowledge into areas of expertise (3–4) that you want to be known for	_____
	☐ You have intentionally identified how your voice and reputation will influence / integrate into the company reputation.	_____
Understand How Others Perceive You, Develop & Deliver a Visibility Plan		
Protect Your Reputation	☐ Ask for feedback on a regular basis from customers, employees, prospects, family, friends	_____
	☐ Googled Yourself, Set up Google alerts on your name	_____
	☐ Developed response scenarios if a crisis happens	_____
	☐ Ask clients and employees for testimonials for your site, Glass Door, etc. (you have a process for positive feedback)	_____

Build Your Reputation	☐ You leverage communication tools (in person, social media, LinkedIn) to share your insights daily, weekly	_____
	☐ You have developed your own frameworks and IP	_____
	☐ You consistently engage with your employees, clients, prospects, community as the face of the company externally	_____
	☐ Your personal brand is consistent across all channels.	_____
Leverage Your Reputation	☐ You leverage your reputation and network to create new opportunities for your business through visibility, partnerships, etc.	_____
	☐ You leverage your voice to give the company a face, engage the employees, and communicate with the industry.	_____
	☐ You are visible in the broader industry and seen as a leader.	_____
Total Points	**If points total less than 150, reach out and read on for help.**	

CHAPTER 1

Why Do Entrepreneurs
Need a Personal Brand?

"Branding demands commitment; commitment to continual re-invention; striking chords with people to stir their emotions; and commitment to imagination. It is easy to be cynical about such things, much harder to be successful."

SIR RICHARD BRANSON

First, you are awesome. It takes a lot of guts to consider launching a business and even more to begin investing in yourself and your idea to move it closer to reality. From the beginning, when you have the idea of a solution, of a company, it is important to ground your solution and make your business personal. Giving a face to a company is critical to connecting and being relevant to your customers — from the start of your idea to your launch, and beyond. If you are out of sight, you are out of mind, and that is death to a new business.

Here are a *few key reasons why your personal brand matters*, especially in the beginning.

1. Your story is critical to connecting with people and getting visibility

2. It is you who makes your company unique and positions you to compete with more clarity

3. Successful companies have cultures that connect with their key stakeholders; many corporate cultures mirror the values and beliefs of the CEO & Founder (think Tony Hsieh[1] and Zappos)

4. Your personal brand can set you apart as a thought leader and an expert in your field — credibility is critical

5. The more positive and intentional your visibility is in the market, the better prepared you are if some setback occurs or negative publicity arises. Whether it is one complaint on Yelp, or an article that paints you in a bad light, or worse, a great personal brand can help protect (at least mitigate the downside) you and your company in bad times.

6. Your reputation is an asset and can be managed (or not) to generate returns, be neutral, or damaging

Your Personal Brand is How You Deliver on Your Promise

Understanding your personal brand, reputation, and how others see you is a critical step in the process of launching your business. Understanding how to blend your personal promise with the new company you are launching makes for a powerful and well positioned business.

When we think about the personal brand, there is still some confusion around what it is and how it interacts with corporate or business branding. It has only just started to be understood by people over the last few years, although I still have clients who have not heard the phrase. It can be challenging to think about ourselves as brands. As people, aren't we are more than just a product, a logo, a set of colors?

Your personal brand is:

1. How you show up

2. How others perceive you

3. What value you bring to the table

4. Helping people know why and when they need you

Here are some examples of CEOs with outstanding personal brands who were able to leverage both their personal brand and company brand to stand out, connect with people, lead their teams forward, and make an intentional impact.

- Steve Jobs and Apple: Visionary, Innovative, Provocative Design, Leader

- Oprah Winfrey and HARPO: Inspirational, Women's Empowerment, Charitable

- Tony Hsieh and Zappos: People-focused, Culture Champion, Delivering Happiness

- Richard Branson and Virgin: Risk Taker, Entrepreneur, Innovative

- Angela Merkel, first woman Chancellor of Germany: known fondly as "Mutti" or Mommy since she is the steady guardian of the nation

- Marc Benioff and Salesforce: Innovator, Disrupter, Philanthropist (launched the 1/1/1 model, 1% of profits, 1% of equity, and 1% of employee hours to the communities it serves)

- YOU: What words would describe you?

We hear about these great personal brands all the time, which is inspirational. This book is about exploring entrepreneurs who are a bit closer to where you might be on your journey. These "reputation rich" CEOs can seem so successful as to be out of reach. However, there is a lot that can be learned from them when it comes to personal branding, insights you can use right now from the beginning. Your new business could be the next Facebook, and getting your personal brand right from the start can help.

As the Face of the Firm, Your Reputation Positions the Company to Compete

Over the last 15 years, the Internet has grown exponentially, and information is consumed at an astonishing rate and is created just as easily — with the touch of a button. Business owners have so much more complexity now when it comes to creating awareness, building new relationships, maintaining current relationships, and figuring out how to stand out in a crowded market. Entrepreneurs have to manage his or her personal brand on a consistent and intentional basis to compete. How a leader shows up and builds trust with their customers and employees is critical.

Let's face it, we all have a brand whether we want one or not. Each person already has a reputation, a calling card, and a way they make people feel. How would people describe you if you were not in the room? When someone mentions your name, how do others think of you? Your reputation is that promise that precedes you, what someone will get when they work with you. For leaders, it is that promise of a vision, for a business owner it is the face you give to a company. People trust and buy from people, not just a company anymore.

Successful CEOs Leverage Personal Branding to Connect & Be Relevant

Many CEOs who I have talked with and worked with start off thinking that they do not want to build their brand because that means you have to be visible and talk about yourself, which seems like bragging. Who wants to be seen as the one running around beating their chest at how wonderful they are? Well, some people do, but most of you don't. There could also be concerns about privacy and, of course, the big concern is around time. How do you find time to manage your personal brand as well as the business? This is a great question and one you will get the answer to in this book. In short, it is about being intentional and aligning your personal brand to support business goals with clear metrics and impact.

Successful CEOs can engage in person and online in ways that add to the reputation of the company and enhance the company brand. CEOs who complement the company brand can get the most bang for their buck and find the best balance of visibility and impact.

Mark Zuckerberg Makes Business Personal with His Drive to Connect

Mark Zuckerberg is a prime example of someone who is focused on his personal brand as an amplifier for Facebook, not a detractor or a distraction. His personal brand hits on the key points we mentioned earlier — it tells his story, his values, and showcases what matters to Facebook through personal experiences. The genius of it is that he leverages his own company platform — Facebook — to engage with fans, customers, and answers questions and comments in a real, authentic way.

From how he dresses, with his trademark gray T-shirt, to how he uses Facebook, and how he spends his time, Mark Zuckerberg has a clear vision for his personal brand. He's a person more interested in relationships than appearances, a trailblazing genius more interested in moving fast in the market than corporate red tape, etc.. Personal branding expert, William Arruda, says that what you wear is critical to your personal brand. "They wear what they wear because that's what they feel comfortable wearing," he says. "When you wear something that just feels right, you are confident. And it is also great to have a trademark look. It makes you memorable and distinctive."[2]

When looking at how Mark Zuckerberg uses Facebook, he shares content that is authentic and in many cases highlights vulnerability as well as his vision for the future. What you share reflects who you are, what you are about, and creates an opportunity for you to connect emotionally with customers. When we think about moving people from the status quo to making a decision, it is a decision made from the heart, not the mind. Mark shares stories about his family, events that have happened personally, and even how he works with employees when traveling. These stories help make him and Facebook be more human, more approachable, more relatable.

Your personal brand is a reflection of what is important to you. Where you spend your time shows people what matters to you too. One example is when Mark learned Mandarin and gave his first Q&A session in Mandarin in 2014.[3] Not only did Mandarin help him communicate with his wife Priscilla Chan's family, but it also highlighted his commitment to learning and the importance of China to Facebook's business. He humbly confessed how horrible his Mandarin was at that 2014 Q&A session, which just made him more human. Only one year later, Mark impressed everyone with his 20 minute speech (in pretty good Chinese) at Tsinghua University in Beijing on October 24th, 2015. After the speech, he shared the video on his own Facebook page. For the first time, he shared how he started thinking about Facebook's mission initially and how it helped him through challenging times.

Your Personal Brand IS the Company Brand in the Beginning

You are not Mark Zuckerberg. However, there is no denying that he had a starting point too. In the beginning, his name was the brand of the company. When you start your company, it is your reputation that gets the company going until it has its brand. It is critical from the beginning to understand what you stand for, what your personal brand is and how that shows up in your company. The more clarity you have on your promise of value, on your own why, the more compelling you can be when you need to connect with your first customer, investor, partner, and more.

Not only should the CEO have a brand, but he or she must outwardly and proactively share it, by having an overt presence on the company's website and social media, for example. Looking at the Weber Shandwick report, *The Social CEO: Executives Tell All*[4], one of the interesting data points was that the non C-Suite executives surveyed thought that:

- Seeing the CEO on social media made the company seem 76% more innovative.

- 57% of those surveyed thought that the CEO's presence on the company website enhanced credibility in the market.

- In addition, 57% thought that the more the CEO was present on the intranet (the internal internet), the more attractive it was to work at that company.

- 75% of those surveyed also said that the CEO gave a company a human face or personality when using these various social platforms.[5]

CEOs Should Build Good Will to Buffer the Challenging Times

It is just as important to understand how your personal views will shape your business decisions. Can you separate your personal views from your customer's views? Do you need to? Here is one scenario, where personal views created issues for the company brand. Chick-fil-A CEO Dan Cathy made headlines[6] in July 2012 when he said he was "guilty as charged" when asked if the company was in "support of the traditional family." What Cathy thought was an innocuous statement, in fact led to a boycott of the restaurant chain by people who support marriage equality.

Since then, Dan Cathy has been interviewed by the Atlanta Journal-Constitution where he stated that "Every leader goes through different phases of maturity, growth and development and it helps by (recognizing) the mistakes that you make," Cathy told the AJC. "And you learn from those mistakes. If not, you're just a fool. I'm thankful that I lived through it and I learned a lot from it."[7] Although this sounds like he learned from this experience, it was not much later that he would also tweet "Sad day for our nation; founding fathers would be ashamed of our generation to abandon wisdom of the ages re: cornerstone of strong societies"[8] in June when the Supreme Court struck down the Defense of Marriage Act. The tweet was deleted; however it was still seen, the damage done.

The challenge with deciding to be visible is that your personal views as a CEO may not align with those of your customers, vendors, employees, and potential customers. Be clear when you think about engaging online (or in person) that what you say, type, video, etc. will be in the court of public opinion, and the digital jury is quick to act and not very forgiving. Think ahead to these questions and understand how differences between your personal views may impact who you decide to serve and also when you communicate your personal brand, what the consequences (good or bad) might be for you and your business.

The Opportunity Cost of Opting Out vs. Gaining a Competitive Edge

These stories should not scare you, yet they should simply remind you to engage in a more intentional way when it comes to your personal brand. The answer is not to stay quiet, there are compelling reasons for engaging and not just defaulting to the status quo of silence. Many CEOs do not believe they need to be visible on social media because so much of their business is done via word of mouth. But with time come new audiences, and the demographics of consumers, talent, and the overall audience is shifting. Millennials are making up more and more of the work-force and have the purchasing power. Also, it's important to be online due to greater reach — you can be in front of anyone with the click of a mouse or the swipe of an app.

Engaging online is no longer optional, it is a critical way to stay relevant. Weber Shandwick and KRC Research published *The Social CEO: Executives Tell All*[9] in 2014, a follow on to their 2012 audit of the online engagement activities of the world's top CEOs (Socializing *Your CEO II*) and continue to see a rise in CEO sociability year over year. The sociability increased from 36% to 66% between 2010 and 2012 and it has risen even more since then. This report was a result of surveying 630 professionals from managers to the C-Suite, excluding CEOs, on the sociability of CEOs. The report covers North America, Europe, Latin America and Asia Pacific, and companies included had revenues of over $500 million.

For CEOs in this Social CEO report, being social means being online in many different ways and getting their word out through internal and external channels. To be out of sight, out of mind for your employees, customers, etc. is typically not the place you want to be when it comes to your reputation and business. If you are not intentionally engaging your different audiences, someone else is. Who else is talking or what you can think of as "taking up oxygen" and getting the attention of your audience?

Investing in Your Audience to Build Trust in You, the Leader, and the Logo

In the HBR Article "Why Trust Matters More Than Ever for Brands" (Prahalad, 2011), by Deepa Prahalad, he discusses forces at play that inform why trust and reputation are important elements of branding. His core message is how "trust is not just a nice to have, but a critical strategic asset." [10]

When companies make decisions, it is a reflection of their leader, which is why it is critical for CEOs to take "brand-stands." [11] A CEO can decide to be a noisebreaker and not just another noisemaker, or just be out of sight and quiet. What has changed over time is how linked the reputation of a company is to that of a CEO, and consumers have noticed. "A full two-thirds (66 percent) of consumers say that their perceptions of CEOs affect their opinions of company reputations. Executives, like consumers, do not overlook the importance of a leader's reputation — they attribute nearly one-half (49 percent) of a company's overall reputation to the CEO's reputation. Executive leadership is critical to burnishing the overall reputation of organizations today, particularly when it is estimated that 60 percent of a company's market value is attributed to its reputation."[12]

Given that consumers have lost respect for CEOs in the US by 72% over the last few years, intentionally managing your brand as a CEO can create a competitive advantage provided it is complementary to the company brand and does not necessarily overshadow it. The tension between the company brand and the CEO's personal brand is a tightrope and should be thought of as two sides of the same coin where balance and integration is optimal. In some cases when the CEO is out in front of the company brand like Mark Zuckerberg, it makes it easier for the company to weather hard questions, customer feedback, and potential reputational challenges. Since most entrepreneurs are so busy in their daily work, it is hard to gather positive feedback proactively from clients before you need it. Negative reviews on Yelp should not be the trigger for the desire to gain positive reviews. You want to build a positive brand bit by bit, interaction by interaction. Build your reputation before you need it.

Now that you understand the importance of a personal brand for a CEO, Founder or Entrepreneur, how do you go about it? Let's start with putting some of your ideas on paper. One key thing to do is to understand how you see yourself, what values are most important to you, so that this can form the foundation for your reputation strategy.

This exercise, called the "Five by Five," is intended to just get the juices flowing. Think of five words that are important to you that make up your reputation and then think of five words that reflect your personal values.

EXERCISE
Five by Five

Pick 5 Words To Describe You	Pick 5 Values That Matter Most To You

This exercise is just the beginning of building the foundation of your personal brand. It is critical that your values and how you want to show up are understood to help inform decision-making about every facet of your business moving forward.

CHAPTER 1 SUMMARY

Your Personal Brand Sets the Tone for Your Business

When you develop your first communication, whether it is your elevator pitch, your first business card, or your first social media post, it should be grounded in your mission and your voice. Building your own personal brand can help build thought leadership that sustains and scales your business by creating more awareness and sets you apart as an expert. Throughout the book you will acquire tools to help you with all of this, with an eye towards efficiency, since you only have so much time in a given day. The more you plan your work and work your plan, the better your odds of getting the most out of your personal brand to move the needle on your business.

CHAPTER 2

Incorporating Your Personal Brand into Your Business

"Do not go where the path may lead, go instead where there is no path and leave a trail."

RALPH WALDO EMERSON

In the last chapter we discussed why you started your business, now we can dive into how to infuse your personal brand, values, and strengths into your company. This includes deciding what you name your company, and once you do, you will have a better sense of how much your personal brand will be the company brand, and thinking through how your reputation should help grow the visibility of the company. When sizing up the competition, be sure to look at the personal brand of the CEO as well as the company brand. Who are the respected thought leaders in the industry and how have they tackled the personal brand and company brand question?

Since starting your own company, you may or may not realize how much you're purposefully engaging with the business but it's really critical to take an inventory to see if you're a visible leader and how much of your brand is facing the market. You will be competing on two fronts — your personal brand and also the brand of your company. Understanding other thought leaders and how they align with their company brand is an important part of this section.

It is important to understand your personal brand and your company brand as two separate entities. We need to know where both brands are for the good of the business. Both brands should align to support the business goals as you look ahead and think about the opportunities and challenges facing the organization. In this chapter, we provide a 2x2 framework to help you assess where you think your personal brand is relative to the company brand. In the below illustration we highlight various ways to think about and assess your brand versus the company brand and what circumstances may be involved. *Where are you on this 2X2?*

ILLUSTRATION
Personal Brand vs. Company Brand: Finding the Right Brand Balance

	Weak — Company Brand — Strong	
Personal Brand — **Strong**	• Serial entrepreneur — new venture • Executive/Professional with great networks outside of the company which allows them to grow their company more quickly with an established reputation • Executive within a company, represented company at events, tradeshows, speaker	• Where a CEO and company brand complement each other • Clarity on business goals and what CEO should highlight vs. company • Well known leader brought into a strong company as CEO
Personal Brand — **Weak**	• New entrepreneur with a great brand within a company as a performer but no network / reputation with knowledge of him or her • Entrepreneur who is an introvert and not sure where to start • Potentially a recent graduate, younger entrepreneur focused on building credibility in many ways	• Big brand with lots of CEO transition, hard to have consistency • Company brand overshadows the CEO • CEO is intentionally not visible • Franchise situation • Company launched pre-internet / social media and the CEO has to decide if they want to catch up
	Weak — **Company Brand** — Strong	

Your Reputation is the Company's Reputation (Especially in the Beginning)

Think about the first time you go to meet a prospect and introduce yourself. It is your ability as the face of this new company to connect and convince others to part with their resources, a.k.a. their money and time, to work with you. Although there are a lot of things you are doing to launch your business — naming it, producing appropriate business cards, going to events, deciding on if it is an LLC, launching a website — when push comes to shove, your ability to get people to trust you and want to do business with you is what makes the fundamental difference. No one knows your company; they only have you as evidence to help them make a decision about working with you.

As you start your company, it is your reputation that launches it. At this point, this new company has no brand, no emotional connection other than what YOU bring to the table. As you define your brand, your story, your purpose more clearly, the strength of your personal reputation will show through and resonate with your prospects. When you think of things that go together with great clarity and purpose, like peanut butter and jelly, or mac and cheese, this is how your personal brand should resonate with a potential client. It should be so clear that you are an obvious solution they should consider because your pitch, your introduction, your compelling case all make it easy for them to think of you and understand why you are their perfect complement to help solve their business problem, and why they want to work with you and not someone else.

Successful entrepreneurs are those who have identified their purpose and have great clarity on their message. It is critical to understand the skills and strengths you can bring to bear for your business and how you position yourself to matter to your audience and increase the relevancy of your business. At the end of Chapter 1 you wrote down your key words that make up your personal brand as well as your values. How do those show up in the company you are creating? One of the first critical tests is thinking about your company name.

Whose Name is It Anyway?

Naming your business is like naming your child. I remember when my husband and I were thinking about names for each child we considered things like: is it unique enough but not too unique, will it grow with our children over time, what is the connotation of the name, and will people make fun of their names. We really liked one of the names, but the acronym was WAD. No one wants that as a name. So we did tweak it, and some day my son will thank me for thinking that through.

Naming your company is just as important, and just as challenging. Your company name is an opportunity to help reflect your values, expertise, and create a great first impression with your clients. It should support your business goals over time and be able to grow with your company while connecting with the audience you are serving. Your business name sets the foundation for your business moving forward, it is the first thing people see on your website, your business card, your social media, and it is what you say when you introduce yourself as the owner. You want to love your company name as much as your customers will.

What are you hoping your name conveys to your audience? Ideally, it is great to have a name that conveys what you do and not a generic name where it is not clear and makes it even harder to figure out what you do. Let's face it though, it is hard to name a company and it always seems like every name is taken, which is one reason why a lot of people starting out just default to their name. There are some good reasons to use your own name and some potential pitfalls you may not have thought about yet.

Your Name is a Great Idea! Right?

Once you decide on the company concept you are launching, then the question becomes how much of you shows up in the company. Are you visible and a large part of the brand? Or are you behind the scenes? When entrepreneurs name a company after themselves it could be done for several reasons. Let's examine these and see what resonates with you. This is a critical first step in aligning your brand and positioning you and your company for success.

Top Reasons to *Name Your Company after Yourself*

1. You want to be a solopreneur and highlight your skills (ex: John Smith Photography or if you want to be a writer, consultant, or a speaker)

2. You are in an industry where names are commonly used (think law firms, accountants, etc.)

3. You want to use your name to make it easy for people to find you online (search engine optimization)

4. You want to create a family business and have a legacy to pass down to your family

5. Maybe you can use your name in a clever way, that has lasting power

6. Your name has legitimate recognition and you can transfer that to your company

7. You could also decide to use your initials and include a key word(s) to make up your company which could be a way around the naming challenge.

8. It is just too hard to find a name (this is possible; however, if this is your answer, dig deep, and keep trying)

There are also some consequences to keep in mind and just acknowledge with eyes wide open. These are important to think about now before you choose to use your name as the new company name.

Top Reasons *Not to Name Your Company after You*

1. It paints the company as a one person show, which may not be the right choice to engender confidence in your clients (especially if you are looking to work with larger companies)

2. If you want to sell your company at some point, you may not want to name the company after you because that implies you are the value and not the company

3. If there are multiple founders, that can be challenging if a partner leaves (or joins)

4. Your reputation is now that of the company, for better or worse

5. Your name likely will not provide insight on what you do and it will require you to communicate your value through your logo, tagline, messaging, etc.

6. If your reputation is known in a certain industry and you pivot to something else, your name may make it hard for your new business to resonate. Let's say you switch from being an accountant to being focused on health and wellness, your name may hurt that pivot versus just choosing a new company name. At best your name may make it confusing to the customer.

Changing your name later can be confusing, expensive, and very challenging, which is why this is one of the initial questions you want to answer very intentionally. Let's talk through what choosing a new name for your company (that is not your name) looks like. There are challenges here, too.

Choose a Meaningful Company Name that Aligns with Your Personal Brand

If you are not sure where to start, think about the words that you associate with yourself, company, products, services, and your customers. For BrandMirror, those words included self-reflection and branding (and lots of other words), that ultimately led to the selection of my company name. Brainstorm names like crazy by yourself, with friends, family, customers, and potential prospects. You should ask people who fit your target demographic to come to your home (or office, or elsewhere) to brainstorm their ideas and words too. It is critical to gather input on your company name during the process. On a big whiteboard or poster-sized paper, just write down names that come to mind in a more free form style and see if patterns emerge for you. Before you decide to hire someone to help, see what you can come up with on your own first.

EXAMPLE
The "Best Rack Around" Gets Naming Right

Recently I was at a Loudoun County Chamber Small Business of the Year[13] event in Loudoun County, Northern Virginia, and several amazing companies were recognized. The one that stood out the most was the one with a great name and an even better story. The retail store, was a finalist for the 2015 Best Retailer category, is called "Best Rack Around",[14] is owned by Nanette Parsons, and is focused on "finding the best fitting bra for your body type". Did you notice that Best Rack Around is B.R.A.? Plus, here is their website description: *Specializing in high-quality and unique-use bras and bra fittings. B.R.A. carries fashion, bridal, maternity, nursing, athletic, mastectomy and post-surgical bras in sizes ranging from A — M cup.* They have a wonderful atmosphere, tagline, and description — it all aligns back to the name and purpose of the company.

Clarity on Your Value & Skills is Key to Naming Your Business

One of the most critical elements to defining your business is to define exactly what you are offering and the pain points you are addressing with your solution. Your name may come directly from your work, especially if you have a product based company. If you have a service based company it can be more challenging to develop your name in such a way that it is unique and clearly illustrates what your business does.

One of my clients, Donna Hoffman[15], is currently working on launching a new venture. A large part of our work has been centered on her personal brand and how that can help her launch her next opportunity. She is already known for helping women get on the first tee faster through Women on Course, a national organization, encouraging women to network through golf. Her business is literally about helping women grow their network and become comfortable on the golf course. However, she is growing her own speaking business and is launching that under her name. One of the key exercises we went through was thinking about what her key skills are, and we defined her key customer segments (and their pain points) in parallel to choosing a name. Although she could certainly use her name, there may be variations of that or a new name altogether that would resonate more effectively with her target market. Once we decided on our top 3 options, we needed to see if they were available before moving forward.

Make Sure Your Name is Viable

One of the best resources you can use is Knowem.com for finding what names are available and even worth investing more time in before getting a logo designed. Knowem[16] checks the availability of the name, social media, and domain name too. Also, you can check if the name is trademarked. It makes it easier to start with using your name consistently everywhere. That moment when you start searching for a name that you like, and you realize that most names are taken, it starts to get frustrating very quickly. It can be hard, so do your best to make it fun and develop a bit of a thick skin when asking for feedback from your customers. Here are some other resources you should check as well, it depends on your situation, but here are some suggestions from the SBA[17]:

- Check for Trademarks, the US PTO has a trademark search tool[18] to check and see if a similar name is used or variations of it

- Check with your state filing office to see if your name has been claimed and is in use

- Make sure your name is domain ready, i.e. available as a domain

- Register your business name by doing a DBA (Doing Business As)

- You can also apply for trademark protection as well (it protects names, words, symbols, and logos that distinguish goods and services)

Also, research names of competitors, too. It is important that your company stands out and not just be another version of the same style of the name of competitors. This initial competitor pass is relatively easy and helps you understand what others are doing when it comes to their branding, website, products, marketing, and services. This research also helps ground what you are offering and how that is unique and different. You personally bring something that is not like everyone else, it is simply a question of being very clear on what market niche you want to connect with and not trying to serve everyone.

The naming decision was one that was an important decision for my business. Originally I named my company Vaughn Advisors (because I had no idea what I wanted to call it yet, I just knew I wanted to get started, so I used my middle name) and then after a few months of being thought of as a financial advisor I realized how urgent it was that I decide on a name. Nothing highlights challenges with a name more quickly than introducing yourself and having someone think you are in the wrong industry.

Choosing a name that reflects the intention of your company, your values, and your purpose makes it easier for you as a founder to be credible and believable every time you go to introduce yourself. You need a company name that you love and that you are proud of wearing. Even though the company may not be named after you, the name is grounded in your beliefs and sets the stage for your company's clarity and success.

One additional element to consider when naming your company is to think about the markets you are entering and how your name translates. Everyone has heard about classic cases like the Chevy car NOVA, which in Spanish means "no go"[19]. Make sure your company name works across cultures, languages, and takes into account religious identities too.

When I incorporated and trademarked BrandMirror I did enlist the help of an attorney, Justin Laughter of Threshold Counsel PC[20], although you can do it on your own for a few hundred dollars as well. I just wanted to be sure I did everything correctly and so worked with a recommended business attorney. Kick off this part of the process sooner rather than later as it can take a while.

Decide Strategically Where to Infuse & Leverage Your Personal Brand

There are several ways to think about where you decide to engage and leverage your personal brand to support your business goals. Here is a simple framework to help you think about goals your personal brand could and should support to enhance the company brand. There may be networks, social media channels, relationships, writing, staff meetings, and more that you as the CEO can leverage to augment the company brand. If you know going in that you are an introvert, think about ways to intentionally and strategically support your company. Don't go to networking events to meet everyone. Instead go to meet a target group of people. Once you accomplish that, go home and relax. We will get into more details later, but that said, early on at least think about this and understand where you may need help versus where you will excel. It is important to go in with at least an idea of how you want your personal brand to stand out.

ILLUSTRATION
Where to Leverage Your CEO Reputation vs. the Company Reputation

Goals	Company Brand	CEO Reputation
Driving Awareness of the Business	*Sponsorships, Advertising, Social Media*	*Speaking, Panels, Networking*
Engaging Current Clients	*Client Appreciation Events, Great Service*	*Personal thank you notes*
Developing New Relationships	*Lunch N' Learns, Webinars, Videos*	*Events, Networking, Sponsorships, Speaking*
Thought Leadership & Influence	*Social Media, White Papers, Case Studies*	*Speaking, Panelist, Author, Blogging, Video, LinkedIn, Social Media*

There is Never Only One

It is important to identify other leaders who are in the space you are looking to occupy and have credibility in their field. Maybe they are big competitors, maybe not, either way it is about understanding who is engaging the audiences that need your solutions to solve their challenges. Your personal brand will need to stand out and be different to connect and resonate. It is not about copying, it is about keeping your finger on the pulse of key topics relevant to your target customers and deciding what you want your role to be in the market and industry.

Identify the visible individuals in the industry you are getting into and understand where they are visible, what they are talking about, and if possible how they are perceived. Do they have negative feedback, are their customers engaged, what is their story when it comes to branding? We will visit this topic again with you, however initially it is important to understand this so that you are informed before you start making serious decisions about your company name, etc. There are several ways to research thought leaders, here are some ideas to get started:

- Search for key phrases on Google and LinkedIn, here are some business examples.

    - "air conditioning expert"

    - "crowd funding"

- "generational wealth management"

- "yoga for kids"

- Top "_____" in your market (dentist, doctor, lawyer, accounting firm, consulting firm)

- Search on Twitter using the #hashtag function. Go to Twitter and enter in key words with a hashtag and see which items are most popular to identify who is talking about them the most. A hashtag is a way to track a conversation, or "tag" it and follow it. Below are some examples for reference.

    - #genderequity

    - #financialinvestments

    - #millennials

    - #entrepreneurship

    - #personalstylist

This chapter is about reflecting and taking action on these key questions:

1. What names have you thought of so far? What are the pros & cons for your company name?

EXERCISE
Company Name Brainstorming Table

Names	Pros	Cons

2. How do you see your personal brand helping the business?

EXERCISE
Identifying How Your Reputation Augments the Company Reputation

Goals	Company Brand	CEO Reputation
Driving Awareness of the Business		
Engaging Current Clients		
Developing New Relationships		
Thought Leadership & Influence		

3. Who are thought leaders in your space?

Identify Thought Leaders in Your Area

Thought Leaders	Company	Areas of Expertise

CHAPTER 2 SUMMARY

Naming Your Business; Thinking About Your Role as CEO

After these exercises, you should have more clarity on the naming options. Also, now is the time to begin thinking about how your personal brand will augment or complement the company brand across those four dimensions we provided. Then, before you jump too far ahead into identifying what is unique about you, it is critical to assess the thought leaders in your market and go in eyes wide open on their messaging, value, and positions. These exercises are to help you learn more about the market and where you fit before you invest too much in your business.

CHAPTER 3

Know Yourself

> "At the center of your being you have the answer:
> you know who you are and you know what you want."
>
> **LAO TZU**

You have thought about your reputation and how your values, skills, and strengths are the foundation and launch pad for your business. This chapter is about exploring your past to get clear on what got you here and what is next. You may be very clear about the nature of your business and why you are starting it. However, if you have not mapped out key moments in your past that have brought you here, now is where we start that process. Being fully self-aware before you jump in and start your business is a critical step. This introspection and reflection provides you with real insight into how you display yourself and your product or service, as well as shape how others perceive you. It is where we will create your personal leadership statement and use that as a way to ground you and ensure alignment with your business and target segments.

What Key Moments Led You Here?

Looking back, think of five to ten memories that are pivotal moments (for better or worse) and have shaped you. These memories might be short glimpses into your past where you remember a feeling or a longer event that you recall much more clearly. The point of this exercise is to find common threads that show up in your life which form the basis of your values, beliefs, strengths, and passions...the very qualities and tenants that make you an entrepreneur.

One of my clients, Judy Redpath, Founder of VISTA Wealth Strategies LLC, spent the first part of her career in high technology and business consulting. It was only after her mother passed away suddenly and unexpectedly that she started her wealth management and financial planning business. After experiencing how challenging it was to help her father settle her mother's estate, and fund and manage trusts, she launched a business to help families think about, grow and manage their wealth and all of the complexities that entails. Look back over your life, into your childhood, when you identify which stories make up your journey.

EXERCISE
Reflecting on Your Journey;
Identifying Moments That Shaped You

Memory / Inflection Point	How has this shaped you?
1.	
2.	
3.	
4.	
5.	
6.	
7.	
8.	
9.	
10.	
Overarching Patterns	

What are the themes that show up? Resilience, creativity, interest in technology? Or maybe there was one inflection point or moment that highlights your pivot to where you are now. What patterns show up for you? These moments are evidence of your choices and journey along the way to where you are today. These experiences that maybe did not seem aligned before, in retrospect, may make sense based on this new venture you are launching. Stepping back to see the forest for the trees is critical to finding the common thread and story that defines the choice you made to launch this business.

Understanding How You are Different

As you think about building your personal brand, your reputation, it revolves around the ability to understand how you see yourself, as well as understanding how others see you as well. In the first chapter, you wrote down five words to describe yourself as well as your values. When you think about what makes you unique from other leaders / competitors, what would you say?

This is one of those moments where it is critical that you think about what makes you truly unique. It could be a myriad of things, here are some ideas:

- What skills you bring together to solve problems for your clients

- Your direct experience could relate to your clients

- You have a distinct solution or framework that has not been created before

- You bring a capability that is not available to most in your industry

Write down what makes you stand out, what others cannot offer that only you can, reference your values and descriptors from Chapter 1 to ensure alignment.

EXERCISE
Five By Five, Identifying What Makes You Unique

Pick 5 words to describe you	5 Values	What ability makes me unique?
Ex: Confident	Ex: Integrity	Ex: Visualization of Concepts

What Do Others See When They See You?

Getting feedback is one of the scariest things for most people, even though it is so important. Instead of waiting for performance reviews, you can make it really easy. Pick a few friends, family members, peers, and ask them to describe you in five words. A great way to do this is to offer to take them out for coffee, lunch, whatever makes it comfortable. Set expectations ahead of time that you are just doing a check in to understand how others see you and that you value their input as you look ahead for the year. Some of them may not know you are starting a business, so if you do not want to disclose that, it is ok. The main purpose is to get their insights — positive and constructive. Ask them to share a few things they like, what they think you do well, and then ask them for one piece of constructive feedback.

EXERCISE
Perception Assessment

Audience	5 Words to Describe You — by Peers, Etc.
Ex: Your Client or a Leadership Team Member	Approachable, Innovative, Humorous, Great Speaker, Resilient

This exercise is interesting, as it gives you a sense of how others perceive you and typically there is a fair amount of overlap between people's feedback. That said, there are always a few surprises that may help you understand where you need to focus on either exploiting that perception or fixing it. If you have worked with a few clients as part of a pilot of your services/minimum viable product, definitely get their feedback if possible.

The reason this feedback approach is helpful is that it is not intimidating. There are some great tools available like William Arruda's Reach 360[21] that you can send out to a set of people for feedback that can be immensely helpful.

What Are Your Core, Undeniable Strengths?

So far we have talked about your values, words that describe you, feedback from others, what makes you unique — now let's look at your strengths. There is likely some overlap in the other words you have gathered. Go ahead and write down your strengths below. You may have taken StrengthsFinder[22] to identify your strengths; there are various tools that can help you identify your strengths. StrengthsFinder is an assessment tool (the concept launched with the bestselling book *Now, Discover Your Strengths*[23]). As an entrepreneur, you will have to wear many hats, and you will not be strong in all of the ways necessary. Even if you are unbelievably skilled, the time it takes to learn how to be an entrepreneur is more than you will likely have. One of the most critical factors in success is delegating things you are poor at or only good at — but not great at. It will help your business immensely.

EXERCISE
Know Your Strengths

Strengths	How do these show up in your business?
Ex: Direct	You are able to give honest, yet diplomatic and constructive feedback to your clients

Understanding your strengths matters so you can be abundantly clear to your prospects on what you bring to the table. It includes acknowledging how you like spending your time too. You may be good at something, but that does not mean you like doing it.

What Gets You Motivated vs. Burned Out?

These skills that you leverage have a name. William Arruda calls them motivational skills versus burn out skills[24]. Those skills you have that you could use them all day long and never notice the time passing, those are motivational skills. The skills that you could leverage, but that suck the life out of you are called burn out skills. You may have left your job and decided to start this company to get back to using those motivational skills. What skills show up in each bucket for you?

EXERCISE
Identifying Your Motivational vs. Burnout Skills

Top Motivational Skills	Top Burnout Skills
Ex: Business development, meeting new people, administrative work, writing blogs	Ex: Finances, Computer / technical work, customer administrative work, invoicing

It is important to understand what skills show up for you as you begin to define your business model and what you are working on every day. The more you can use your motivational skills the better, however as an entrepreneur you will absolutely have some burnout skills that will be leveraged or, as mentioned above, outsourced. The skills exercise leads us to the next big question.

How Are You Relevant Today?

When you look at your skills, strengths, and what makes you unique, how does it make you relevant? Do you have any gaps that you need to fill to deliver value to who you believe your customer is? If you are not sure of this answer, at least be open to looking at it on a regular basis. Tom Hayes, Phil Styrlund, and Marian Deegan, wrote a great book called Relevance: Matter More[25] in 2014. The book (Phil Styrlund, 2014) was a insightful read and the formula they outline is powerful.

Relevance = (Authenticity + Mastery ^{2} + Empathy) X Action

Think about this equation, are you clear on how you are authentic and what that means in your business? What about mastery, we talked about skills and strengths, what are you a master of at this point? What is your core expertise? In the next chapter, we will talk about your customer segment, which is where empathy comes in, understanding what pain points your prospects have and how you can help. Then, of course, the last piece — action — what are you doing about it? How are you relevant? Leveraging this formula is a great way to gut check if what you are doing is connecting and mattering. Phil Styrlund also gave a wonderful TEDx[26] talk at TEDxRockCreekPark in 2013. I met Phil and Marian, and was able to review the book before it was published and love this concept of relevance and mattering more.

What is your expertise?

Following on this idea of relevance, let's dive into the concept of having mastery or expertise in a certain area. Think about what your areas of expertise are and write them in the diagram provided. It is important not to be everything to all people. Choose three, no more than four, areas of expertise that you have. Below is an example from Donna Hoffman, founder of Women on Course[27]. These areas or themes were a result of the journey work we did and found consistency and a meaningful thread throughout her life. You have one too.

EXAMPLE
Donna Hoffman — Reputation Rings Exercise

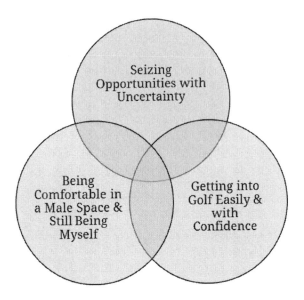

Seizing Opportunities with Uncertainty

Being Comfortable in a Male Space & Still Being Myself

Getting into Golf Easily & with Confidence

These themes are critical in later chapters when we develop thought leadership content, and it provides focus on what you should talk about, which is just as important as helping you understand what not to talk about as well.

Think about what your areas of expertise diagram would look like given the moments that stood out for you, your strengths, skills, and experiences. Feel free to do this on a piece of paper, or here in the book below. This diagram is critical when thinking about your unique value proposition. Because the center of this diagram starts to reflect that uniqueness about you. If you had a hard time defining that before, then seeing it represented in a visual may help. What three areas of expertise do you have? These may show up in your company; they could be transferable skills, or your passions and hobbies. What are you an expert at in your life? The Venn diagram enables you to also see where your strengths overlap and can deliver value in interesting and more complex ways.

EXERCISE
Identify Your Areas of Expertise, Your Reputation Rings

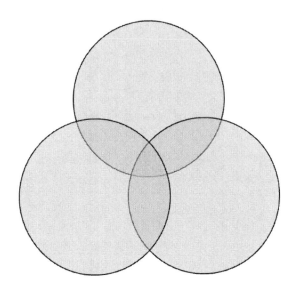

What is Your Vision?

When you thought about creating your company, there was some problem you saw that you wanted to fix. For Donna Hoffman, she had seen first-hand how exclusive golf seemed to women. After traveling all over the country visiting golf courses for work, she also realized that there was no reason for women to not be on the course other than they just needed some help. Her *vision* is as follows:

"To create the power of shared experiences that allows for developing real relationships and skills to move ahead in life and your career leveraging golf to do so"

DONNA HOFFMAN

What is the vision you see for the world when you think about creating your company?

EXERCISE
Defining Your Vision

MY VISION IS:

What is Your Leadership Promise?

Your personal brand is what people expect from you, your promise, how you show up. You are the founder of a company, so what is your promise? The Harvard Business Review had a fantastic article called, "From Purpose to Impact,"[28]written by Nick Craig and Scott Snook, that discusses purpose-driven leadership. One of the fascinating parts of their research (Snook, 2014) is that even though they have trained thousands of managers and executives, they found that fewer than 20% have a strong sense of their individual purpose. CEOs can recite their organization's mission, but had a much harder time articulating a compelling purpose statement when it comes to their own.

Here is one way to think about crafting your leadership purpose, answer these three questions and then develop your statement. 1) What kind of a leader are you? 2) What are you committed to doing? 3) What skills, areas of expertise, are you leveraging to drive the change you are looking for as a leader? If you like filling in the blank, here is your template. When you think about what kind of leader you are, go back to your strengths, and to feedback from others and see what shows up consistently. Are you authentic, approachable, conscientious, or provocative? What resonates for you?

Illustration: Sample Leadership Promise

I am a __ "approachable"_____ leader, who is committed to ____ "changing the world one parent at a time with this new time saving, peace of mind product_, by leveraging my key skills of __ "been there done that as a parent"__, ____organization_____, ____down to earth way of communicating____.

Exercise: Draft Your Leadership Promise

I am an_____ leader, who is committed to _____, by leveraging my key skills of_____, _____, _____ _____.

When you enter in what you are committed to, think about what you want to see happen, and then how you are doing that. Which skills are leveraged the most, particularly ones that are unique to you?

Ideally, this promise statement would work for your life, not just as CEO. For example, Batman and Bruce Wayne have very different promise statements and personal brands. Many clients, before working with BrandMirror, have this split existence where their personal brand is different at home, vs. at work. The intent of this promise statement should be that it applies at any moment in your life. It is what you write down and put on your mirror at home as your mantra. You can share this as a CEO if you like; many CEOs share this with their team as a way to connect more authentically and be more vulnerable. As a gut check, see if this promise statement could be used at any time on any day to see if you are showing up the way you want to in life. If you love it, then you are ready to move forward.

What Promises Are You Making on Purpose?

As you look over your Areas of Expertise Diagram and your Leadership Promise, what is it that you promise your potential customer? When they work with you, what are they going to get in each interaction, from the start of introducing yourself, your website, your proposal writing, your products and services, your personal and marketing communication? Each Interactions is important because it reflects your personal brand showing how you work with your customers. When you think about working with prospects, clients, and partners — which elements are critical to showcasing your reputation and helping you deliver value intentionally?

For example, one of the elements of my leadership promise is to *leverage structured ways to help people find and live their purpose while increasing their impact and visibility.* Meaning that in every workshop, talk, keynote, presentation, book, one on one interaction — I always have a framework, structure, diagram to help people move the needle on their visibility and impact. Partly because I am a visual learner and leverage that skill to help clients. People can find a process and tools very helpful to keep momentum and not get stuck. Whether it is writing your promise statement, bio, resume, or LinkedIn profile, tools help.

CHAPTER 3 SUMMARY

You Know How You are Unique, Now What?

This chapter is about understanding a few key elements that underpin your reputation. The exercises you did here included:

- Creating your Purpose Statement

- Defining your key descriptors and your Values

- Defining Your Vision

- Understanding how others see you

- Defining your Areas of Expertise

It is critical to understand how you see yourself, what you think you are really good at and then how others see you. Understanding that gap, or if things are aligned very well, is important as you look at which customers are your target market. Remember, you do not need to appeal to everyone, you want to have a clear niche and promise to resonate, connect, and be relevant. You can leverage the "Reputation at a Glance" worksheet to capture what comes out of this chapter, as well as chapters 3, 4, and 5.

EXERCISE
Reputation at a Glance

This one-page template can help you see your brand on one page. Write in your ideas as you go through the exercises in the book.

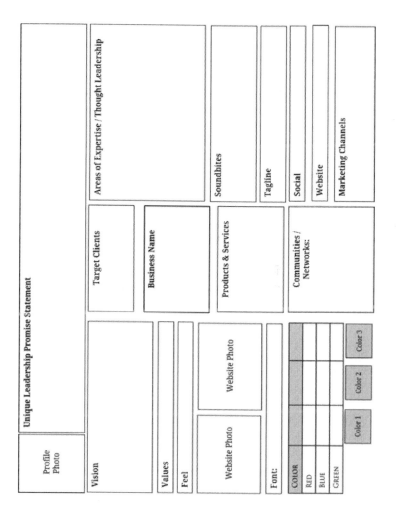

CHAPTER 4

Discover & Know Your Audience

"Your customer doesn't care how much you know until they know how much you care."

DAMON RICHARDS

When you first start your business, it is challenging to know who is willing to pay for your services and how much. Which customers will care about how you are unique, your strengths, and your areas of expertise? One of the most critical missteps for an entrepreneur is not initially piloting services on trusted in-network people, who could be legitimate customers. You know when you start your business that the services and products you have are not perfect, nor should they be perfect. It would be nice, but completely unrealistic to have that happen. Creating your MVP, your minimum viable product, and testing it to help validate and vet your target customers is critical. This includes identifying what is the true pain point and what messaging resonates with your buyer and end user.

It is important to practice your services and products to gather evidence — evidence of what worked and did not work — as well as gaining your own ability to speak with credibility about who you have worked with in the beginning. Understanding how you describe your solution and how people hear it is critical. You may think you know exactly what the customer wants, but have you asked? Have you practiced pitching your solution 10 different ways to see what resonates? The purpose of this chapter is to know your customer, what they need, and be sure before moving ahead. Many entrepreneurs skip this step without validating their customer pain points and it can lead to a lot of heart ache and missed opportunities. Being smart about your solution does not necessarily equate to being great at selling. You may think you know which customers will want your solutions, but it is best to check and ask before building out your website, marketing materials, and investing a lot of time and money.

Who Cares About What Solutions You Have?

Initially, think about the three to five customer segments which have the pain points you are solving for at this point. It is not about you, remember, it is about the customer. It is about understanding who really cares about your solutions. When you start your company it is based on your personal reputation and on your ability to connect with your prospects and be in a constant listening and learning mode.

What target segments do you believe you are serving? Write down the segments in the table below. Be intentional about identifying your end user versus the decision maker, as they could be very different people.

EXERCISE
Identifying Your Target Customers, Their Pain Points, and Decision Makers

Customer Segment	Pain Point	Decision Maker
Ex: Working moms age 30–45	No time to even plan a vacation	Mom, Husband
Ex: Teenage girls	Hate shopping, want their clothes delivered b/c too insecure about self to go out and shop	Mom

When I started, the first thing I wanted to do was build a website, get business cards, and go! Before you start building your website (or anything else), which can be exciting in the beginning, go out and talk to your potential customers and get a sense of whether or not you are accurate in understanding their pain points. It is important to listen to customers and hear what bothers them in their words, not in *your* words. If you talk about your product in a certain way, although it might be true, it might not be at all how the customer thinks about it. However, before we can ask, we have to find your customers.

Where are These Customers?

Do you know where to find your customers? If your target segment includes CEOs where do you start? For example, if you want to find CEOs, they are not typically at networking events because that is not where they spend their time. They might be in leadership programs, attending more senior level events like awards banquets, or they may just be at home after a long day at work. Once you identify your segments, do some initial research to identify where they are. Create a segment profile that includes key demographic information: where they live, how much income they have, where they eat, what they do for fun, and sectors they are in, etc.

Strategies for B2B and B2C Customers

In some cases, your customer could be Business to Consumer (B2C), or Business to Business (B2B), or both. How are you vetting this and then building out the demographic information to find them? One resource you could use for the professionals would be LinkedIn. Whether you are B2C or B2B, LinkedIn helps you identify both based on key words you might find in their profile, location information, job level which could be a proxy for income range, and even job title.

For example, if you were leveraging LinkedIn as a starting point for B2C and B2B, then you may want to build out a segment table to understand what your revenue generating segments look like.

ILLUSTRATION
LinkedIn Customer Segment Mapping Tool

LinkedIn Fields	Segment 1 B2C	Segment 2 B2B	Segment 3 B2B
Brief Description	C-Suite	HR Firms	Advisory Firms
Key Words	CEO, CXO	Training & Development	CPA, Banker, Lawyer
Location (w/in how many miles of you?)	Metro Area	Metro Area / National	Metro Area / National
Industry	What customers need you the most?	Which industry needs you most?	Which industry needs you most?
Company Size	50+	50+	50+
Evidence — how can you confirm your hypothesis?	What will tell you they need you?	What will tell you they need you?	What will tell you they need you?
Value / Pain Point	What are their top pain points?	What are their top pain points?	What are their top pain points?

Utilize in person tools like networking events and online tools like LinkedIn and Google to do high level research.

- Leverage LinkedIn to find individuals in the industry you are looking at to see what groups they are in

- Google the companies you are looking at to find out what events they are at — or who their decision makers are based on your services and products

- Attend Chamber events to get a sense of which industry groups exist and begin to build relationships with potential customers

The above must be done authentically and strategically. If you show up and try to sell someone, that typically may not work, people need to trust you before they do business with you. Get out of your office and attend events to introduce yourself and your company, ask questions to potential customers and listen to understand their challenges. Do not be in a sales mode. Ask how they solve these problems at this point, what has worked or not worked in the past. Connect with people initially without being pushy and slowly nurture and grow your relationships. The most critical thing is to get started with a plan and work your plan. Ask others to help introduce you to the right people as well. Don't be afraid to ask for help.

Discover Networks and Communities Online for Research and Insights

One of the most critical things you can do is research online and identify communities that are your target market. You can start out by looking at sites like:

- Quora[29] (website where you can answer all sorts of questions to build an online presence as an expert)

- LinkedIn[30] groups (research what topics or challenges are being discussed in groups)

- Facebook groups (research what groups exist for your target segment and their discussions)

- Yelp[31] (Research companies like you and the feedback they get online)

- Pinterest[32] (Identify your segment and what they are sharing, what matters to them)

- Instagram[33] (Identify your segment and what they are sharing, what matters to them)

- YouTube[34] (What videos have been made for your customer, what solutions?)

- Competitor sites (Research how your competitors identify and speak to your target customers)

A lot of your discovery will be online research where you are simply listening and looking for pain points in the areas discussed in the previous chapter. These same forums are great for use later when you want to create communities and engage. It is also possible that you can find partner organizations to work with that are complementary to what you are looking to do too. The PEW Research Center published a demographics report in August 2015, "The Demographics of Social Media Users[35]", across the five main platforms: Facebook, Pinterest, Instagram, LinkedIn, and Twitter. The report also shares information on engagement for each of the channels which can help inform your marketing plan and timing of content.

Ask Your Prospects & Customers What Challenges They Face

As you begin to validate your customer segments and have learned enough to have a better sense of who they are, then you can get more methodical about your research. An intentional learning agenda about your customer segments, and how to learn about what elements of your products and services matter the most is important. Specifically, be intentional about what makes you different from others. As you think about moving customers into a place to make a decision, assess your key points against competitors and understand how you stack up and which of those attributes of your solution create differential value.

Moving From Status Quo into Action Means Understanding What Matters Most

Your personal brand is really not about you, just like selling is not about you. It is all about your audience and what they are looking for that is valuable. In this section, we will talk through the various ways a customer may think of value and how your message can capture that value in a compelling way.

According to the Sales Benchmark Index[36], 60% of all possible sales are lost to "no decision", this highlights how much people do not like changing what they are doing. When we think of moving people to change, think of Newton's First Law where he states that "An object at rest stays at rest and an object in motion stays in motion with the same speed and in the same direction unless acted upon by an unbalanced force"[37]. So basically, your solution has to be so jarring, something so compelling, as to move your prospect to decide to work with you. Do you understand what makes your customer tick? It is referred to as psychographics.

It is important to understand who your clients are as people. How does your solution fit into their lifestyle?

Each product or service tends to have 3 levels of value when it comes to positioning: functional, value-add, and emotional. Basically speaking to the basic tasks accomplished, the additional things that make things mentally easier, and then the emotional part which speaks to the heart. When you look at your solutions, how are you doing in each of those areas?

1. *Functional* is just acknowledging what is the no-kidding day to day performance of your product/service. How does it function? It includes the bare minimum performance.

2. *Value Add* is where you start to get into what additional things you (or competitors) do to make the product/service more compelling.

3. *Emotional* is all about how you are making the prospect feel during the process. When they use your product/service does it resonate emotionally, do they have more peace of mind, more confidence, more assurance, relief?

Choose one of your products / services and sketch out the Head to Heart Diagram. You can also look at your competitors through this same lens to assess how you are competing and most importantly positioning yourself effectively.

ILLUSTRATION
Moving Customers Out of the Status Quo, Speak to the Heart

Head to Heart

Value Add. Speaks to the Mind

Example: Your solution saves time because it is simpler than other solutions

Emotional. Speaks to the Heart

Example: Because your solution saves time, it makes this customer feel relieved and more confident in their job

Functional. Speaks to Basics

Example: Your solution should deliver on the core purpose, like ease of use, its intended core function.

Do You Have Messaging that Matters?

Once you are clear on looking at your customer pain points and how you can solve those challenges with messages that fit on the functional, value add, and emotional level, it is time to build your own way of communicating these messages that resonate with each segment. This is where your personal brand is critical to connecting authentically with your prospect. One of the most important keys to connecting is to make it conversational. People typically do not respond to sales tactics. When was the last time you hoped a salesperson would approach you?

Whether you realize it or not, as a solopreneur or CEO you are a sales person and the best sales people connect through "low pressure" listening and conversations. Discovering pithy ways to describe your value as an individual and as a representative of the company means being able to have a short sentence or saying that gets their attention and keeps them interested in wanting to do business with you.

When you have a clear, short message you can communicate your product and service to your target segment in a clever and effective way using as few words as possible. Did you know that people have about an *8 second attention span* and that is down from the year 2000 when they had a 12 second attention span (according to a Microsoft Corp. study[38])?[39] If you cannot get them in your opening with a great first impression in under 8 seconds[40], it can take you multiple times and even months to change the first impression you made.

Here are some examples of pithy phrases, you could also just work on your own short ways to describe your solutions too. These are usually more than a tagline and at most a sentence. Think of these as sound bites. They are your beliefs, discovered earlier when you mapped your journey. They are your own –*isms* that get people hooked on what you are saying and resonate with your target segments. You want to have a short message that works when you are out and about and you can use it in your copy later too, as well as a slightly longer version of your messaging. The examples below are from Maura Fredericks, founder of Thrive with Maura Fredericks[41] (Thrive Consulting & Coaching, LLC). She works with co-founders and their teams to improve how their business runs through better communication.

ILLUSTRATION
Maura Fredericks, Identify Your Sound Bites that Resonate with Customers

- "If you are doing everything, are you doing anything?"

- "Time management should be called decision management"

What are your –*isms*? What do you say that really resonates when you are out talking with potential customers, clients, and partners? Developing an inventory of these sayings can be very beneficial to provide you something memorable to share without selling people something. It is a great way to start a conversation or use an analogy to convey what it is you do to a prospect.

Review & Assess Your Personal & Business Networks Consistently

When you start your company, it seems like organizations come out of the wood work to have you join and grow your business or help validate your business. It could be the Better Business Bureau, Dun & Bradstreet which help validate your business. There are also groups that promise to grow your business like BNI, Chambers of Commerce in your area, alumni groups, religious groups, networking groups like national associations, or other groups. It is important to understand where your prospects and customers are on a consistent basis and also ensure your networks continue to provide you with valuable business. There are several things to consider as you jump in and build your networks.

1. Pick up to five places to invest in and network at in the beginning given where you believe your customers are

2. Try these out before you agree to buy, if possible

3. Keep in mind that the networks you join also reflect your personal brand

4. Ask how the groups work, visibility, events, members, and how they see you contributing value to the group

5. Choose networks that do not overlap much, if at all — avoid the trap of being in the same groups with the same people

6. Consider also the quality of relationships, do you form strong ties or weak ties?

The Network and Small Groups[42] paper discusses the networking concept in greater detail and provides insight into how best to consider constructing your network.[43] They discuss the idea of social capital and how you build that within and across your groups. It is important to understand the social capital you create and also how you deploy it. As the owner / CEO you can deploy social capital in ways that generate value for others, extend your visibility, plant seeds for future relationships and customers, as well as allow you to show up as a leader for your employees. Of course, an easy way to measure value is to track leads, revenue, and profit as well as visibility when it comes to your business and building your personal brand.

Another critical concept from the *Network and Small Groups[44]* paper is around this notion of homophily[45], when you decide to join groups that are like you. We all probably know the saying "birds of a feather flock together", and when it comes to networking be intentional about how similar and different you are to your groups. You may seek to have groups with the same values and yet choose groups that cross industries, have varying seniority levels, and various access to extended networks that you want to penetrate at some point. It is important to surround yourself with diversity so that you can expand your reach to new customers in an optimal way. Every year consider reviewing your networks, removing one and adding one, or at a minimum adjusting your time and recommitting where you see the most return on your time.

Align Your Customer Segments and Growth Goals

It is important to understand how much your customers can pay you. When you look at this idea of payment it is not only what they can afford, but also what they perceive your products or services are worth. In the beginning, you may focus on one product or service as you get started, however the reality is that you will most likely want to build out multiple revenue streams and/or multiple packages with tiered pricing. Look at how much revenue and profit you are looking to make over the next 12 months and then back into how many sales of each of your products or services you need to make. Often solopreneurs forget to recognize how many hours they have and therefore miscalculate how many widgets they will need to sell to make their business work. As you identify your customer segments, be sure to also understand how your segment choices impact your business model.

EXERCISE
Identify 3–5 Revenue Generating Segments & Where They Are

Segment	Network / Location	Products / Services	Annual Revenue	Priority
Ex: Students	Campuses, Sororities	Blow Dry services @$50 a piece	20 a month on season, 5 a month off season Total = $1250X12 =$15K	Low priority
Ex: Professionals	Conferences, associations	Blow Dry services @$100 a piece	20 a month consistently $2,000X12 =$24K	Medium Priority

Evolve with Your Customer

Over time, as your business grows and evolves, it is important to constantly ask yourself if you are meeting your customer where they are. Just as you may re-invent yourself in your career, customers have shifting needs too. Do you have mechanisms in place to let you know proactively or reactively?

ILLUSTRATION
Francisca V. Alonso, Co-Founder and CEO of AV Architects + Builders

Francisca V. Alonso is the co-founder of AV Architects + Builders in northern Virginia. As a second generation architect, her passion is to design and build spaces that create happiness and help her residential clients "love their home again." For over 15 years, Francisca has built a reputation as someone who does the right thing, has a passion for design, believes in cultivating people, and doing all of this with integrity. With an extended team of thirty people, it is critical that her employees and clients feel that her business and how it operates is an extension of her values. Francisca engages with the community through mentoring high school students in her area, to bigger programs like the Hot Mommas Project[46]. As a female in a largely male-dominated industry, she owns her personal brand very intentionally. At events, she brings her signature red construction hat and heels to kick things off. Her business is not a job, it is a mission to help clients bring design intentionally into their homes.

As Francisca has worked with clients over the years, she has evolved her business based on client needs. What started as a focus on renovations has grown to include a specialization in helping her clients "age in place." She has built an entire practice around designing for the baby boomer generation and helping them enhance their space to fit their needs. Her projects include smaller renovations which leverage the "universal design" principle. This means that doors are wider, there are fewer steps, living space on one floor, for example. She even moved her office to Great Falls, VA, right in the middle of where her clients are located. Looking ahead, Francisca is publishing a book on how to design for the baby boomer generation. As for new construction, be on the lookout for her new homes in northern Virginia, specifically designed for baby boomers. According to Francisca, over 70% of baby boomers want to stay in their current neighborhoods, so evolving to help meet their needs is a critical and very intentional move.

CHAPTER 4 SUMMARY

Know Your Target Customer and Their Value

It is critical to know your customer and continually re-visit who they are on a regular basis at the beginning of your business and beyond. You may need to test and learn to ultimately get to the customer segment you want to attract, and then be very intentional on referring the rest and being able to say no. Once you know where your customer is, you can plan how to connect, how to add value through compelling messaging, and continually listen for any changes in their needs. Do not underestimate the time you want to spend investing in networking strategically and intentionally to get visibility and business.

CHAPTER 5

Anchor Your Personal and Company Brand

> "I've learned that people will forget what you said, people will forget what you did, but people will never forget how you made them feel."
>
> **MAYA ANGELOU**

When it comes to building your personal brand, you are defining how you want people to experience you and your company. The key question is how do you want them to feel when they see you, email with you, follow you on social media, and meet with you, etc.? Every interaction is meant to reinforce your unique leadership promise and the value you bring to your customers. This chapter is all about understanding and defining how you want to show up with the company brand, and doing an inventory and assessment of how your personal brand manifests itself in every interaction you have. This section is focused on creating a meaningful impression at every point in the client experience.

Distill Your Key Descriptors & How They Influence the Client Experience

How do you want people to feel when they work with you and therefore your company? Distill the essence of your personal brand into three to five words; here are some that were chosen for a client of mine, Maura Fredericks, founder of Thrive, who is dedicated to coaching co-founders, business owners, and business teams.

- Honest and Progressive — known for telling clients what they need to hear

- No Nonsense — cut to the chase firmly and politely

- Curiosity — always asking questions and wanting to know more

- Provide Clarity — enables focus by creating clarity through questions

- Approachable & Collaborative– easy to talk to, fair and nice

- Energetic — wants to help clients Thrive, feel inspired

These words also align with Maura's leadership promise as well as her tagline too. What is it that you would want people to associate with you? These words can be translated into your company name, the colors, the fonts, and even the photos you decide to use. Every interaction is a chance to make another impression and reinforce your promise. When you think about your promise in relation to your company it is important to understand the intentional overlap.

Getting Clear on Where You as CEO Contribute to the Company Brand

Brainstorm how your key words align with the words used to describe your company. In the below table, think about how you might complement your company's voice. Are there natural places where you align with your company's voice and how you want your clients to describe you?

EXERCISE
Identify Your Key Words and Voice
vs. Your Company Key Words and Voice

Key Words for Your Personal Brand	Key Words for Your Company Brand
Examples: pragmatic, forward thinking, conductor (quiet leader), innovative, loves photography, people person	Examples: creative, energetic, looks ahead for trends, people centric culture

One way to think about your reputation is understanding what you know about, which could fall in one or more of these buckets: your company, skills, or passions. The Venn diagram showcases your reputation visually. In this example, you are a CEO and have a passion for photography, on top of your outstanding leadership skills. How does that show up in your role? Here are two ideas on how this CEO's personal brand could add value to their company and support the business goals.

ILLUSTRATION
Visualizing Your Reputation

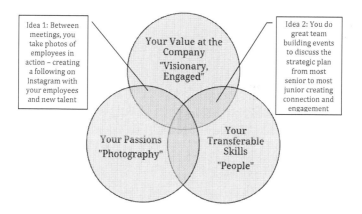

For my clients, leveraging this tool provides a way to visualize their expertise as well as identify overlaps, which is where real magic can happen. The overlap is where topics intersect and can help you differentiate yourself as the CEO to your employees, customers, and beyond.

Brainstorm your thoughts on what you personally would talk about or do vs. the company. Then capture those ideas below. As you list them, it is likely that there is a crossover and there should be. That said, you get to decide how much of your brand influences the company brand. Mapping this out will make what you contribute personally to support the company brand more intentional. In addition, it is the combination of your strengths that helps you be truly unique. Be sure to take into account your business goals as well.

EXERCISE
Identify Your Areas of Expertise and How They Align with the Company Brand

Your Personal Brand	Your Company Brand
Example: Passion for People & Photography — love recruiting	*Example: Company is very people focused with transparent employee practices*

Another way to look at how your personal brand supports the business is deciding what touchpoints will be influenced by your brand. One way to think about the customer experience is considering what their decision making cycle is like. Where you can brainstorm how you show up to customers throughout buying process:

- *Standing Out:* How do they find out about you amidst the noise?

- *Learn through Exploration*: How can they research and consider you?

- *Decide:* Make it easy to do business with you

- *Engage and Spread the Word*: How are you interacting so that the customer spreads the news about you, keeps coming back, and refers others to you?

Even brainstorming this list and choosing a few items per each part of the decision cycle would help you understand where you engage versus the company.

ILLUSTRATION
Where do you, as the CEO, influence the customer's decision to buy?

Decision Stages	Your Personal Brand	Your Company Brand
Standing Out	CEO Blog / Social Media Industry Panels **1st Impression (in person and online)**	Press Releases **Social Media** **Company Website**
Learn & Explore	CEO White Paper	Market Research
Decide to Buy	Thank you phone call	Easy to pay online
Engage & Advocate	Quarterly Check In	Social Media w. news

If you are starting out, there is definitely a prioritization that occurs, however be sure that you re-visit the decision making cycle on a regular basis to assess how you are doing. The bolded examples in the table are a great place to begin. Let's get started with the first impression part of how you show up. As you think about your personal brand, be intentional about how you show up and build relationships with people at networking events, conferences, client meetings. You have one chance to make a great first impression. Now that you know how you are different, it's time to map what that feels like to the customer.

First Impressions Last (a Long Time)

Although we have talked about naming, etc. — you may not be quite there yet, AND you are still out networking. It has happened, I have met new entrepreneurs that do not have a card yet and are just meeting people and learning who is who. If this is the case, here is some data to help explain why first impressions matter so much.

One of the most important things to understand about a first impression is how the brain processes information. Dr. Albert Mehrabian (B.S. and M.S. in Engineering from MIT and a PhD from Clarke University) of UCLA has done research on the importance of verbal and non-verbal communication[47]; he is considered a pioneer in the field of non-verbal communications[48]. His findings highlight that when you walk into a room, people first assess you based on how you look, then your tone, then based on what you actually say. This is known as the *7% (what you say)-38% (how you say it)-55% (how you look) Rule* where Mehrabian says that most communication happens non-verbally with what you actually say making the smallest impact. This research is not the end all be all to communications, however the framework does highlight how visual people are which is relevant when we talk about personal branding. It is critical to understand that how others see you is how they will see your company. Think about how you look, your tone when you engage, and then how you start off the conversation as key to delivering on your personal brand.

Cyndy Porter, Image Consultant: Building an Intentional Image

One of the entrepreneurs I partner with is Cyndy Porter, a professional image consultant. It is critical to think about your image, since it makes such a difference when it comes to your first impression. How well put together you look leads people to have more confidence in you. Cyndy works with clients to help them understand their body type and find clothes that fit their body and their brand. Your first impression takes only 6–10 seconds to make and yet it can take up to 6 months or 7 interactions to fix it. Here are some insights from Cyndy:

- Once you understand your brand and what you wish to convey, think about how you are communicating that in subtle ways through how you dress. For example, if you are creative, how does that show up in the style of clothing you choose, the accessories you wear, your hair and makeup?

- Your personal style is a powerful communication tool. When you dress your personal best it attracts people to you. They will be interested in you, want to meet you, talk with you, work with you, and get to know you.

- When you know you look put together, it boosts your self-confidence, allowing you to focus externally to accomplish great things without self-doubt or awkwardness.

- How you dress can make you more relevant and overcome barriers:

  1. If you are younger and want to be taken more seriously dressing in darker, classic clothing can help you gain respect.

  2. If you are older and worry about being perceived as current, a stylist can help you with your hair, clothes, and makeup so you look modern and on top of your game.

  3. If you are an introvert, knowing you look your best can give you the added confidence to enter a room with presence.

4. If you are sometimes seen as a bit aggressive you can learn to dress in a way that tones down your presence in a more likable manner.

The bottom line is that creating an intentional image can help you achieve success. It's not superficial, it's an extension of who you are and how you present yourself to the world. If you need help identifying your style personality, you can visit Cyndy's website (https://www.cyndyporter.com) and download her free e-book quiz to get a sense for your style.

Getting Started with the Your First Impression Online (Visually and Verbally)

The most important parts of your personal brand materials are what you need to succeed with a great first impression online. These are items that work for you when you are not managing them.

- Your headshot — get a professional photo done

- Photos of you as CEO in action, images that align with your brand

- Evidence of your brand (digitize your brochures, use videos, photos, etc.)

- LinkedIn profile completed

- Social media, if needed

If you have the above we can get started on your email signature, your business card, landing page / website, and even a brochure or flyer. What is also interesting is that people have the same attention span on LinkedIn, after about six seconds on your profile your potential client has already made their decision to move on or to connect with you.

A Profile Picture is Worth Hundreds of Connections on LinkedIn

Many of your first impressions will be in person, however a lot of those impressions will also be what you have online, like your LinkedIn profile. An outstanding headshot goes a long way on LinkedIn, your bio, and other marketing material. With a small investment, get a professional headshot photographer and take head shots in a few different outfits. You may want a suit, something business casual, and then something more relaxed but professional. It is great to have a few versions so you can leverage them in unique and effective ways based on your marketing campaigns, materials, and customer segments. People without LinkedIn profile headshots are skipped over 14X more than someone with a headshot. If one of your goals is to build visibility through speaking, being on panels, etc., you will absolutely need a great headshot. If possible, get a professional photo of you in action: consulting, coaching, teaching, whatever your business is, give people a picture to visualize you doing your thing.

Choosing Your Company Name

Earlier I wrote about your company name and the pros and cons of naming companies after the founder. If you have made a decision, then now is the time to help ensure it aligns with your personal brand and the upcoming steps around tagline, color, logo, etc. Don't forget to look at Knowem.com to identify what names are available and try and get the right social media handles too. The shorter the company name the better, so if you can get your name to between 1-3 words, great. Your company name and tagline will both be hard to create and yet critical to getting your company off on the right foot. Although you can search at the USPTO site, you may want to consider enlisting the help of an attorney when it comes to being sure you protected your new company and that you are not at risk of changing it later because someone else is using it.

Know Your "War Cry", Your Slogan, Your Tagline

Understanding the key phrase and words that go with your brand is important. We all know the Nike tagline, Just Do It. What is your tagline for you? You may have one that is yours and the company tagline, or maybe you have one phrase that you use, for example, on your business card, website, or on LinkedIn. What is a short phrase that captures your essence and commitment? It should be something that is distinct and not easy to copy.

Taglines are challenging to come up with, a good tagline adds to the brand very intentionally. It communicates what the company does simply, how it does it, why it does it, or in some cases to get you to think or take action. Here are a few questions to ask yourself as you think about your tagline.

1. How is the tagline building on to your business identity?

    - TED: Ideas worth spreading (it helps explain what TED is)

2. What is it telling / asking people to do?

    - Nike: Just Do It (commanding)

3. As the solopreneur, you might have your own "tagline" or name

    - Jane Smith: The _____ Guru (just be careful with making your own tagline, you have to back up whatever you declare)

4. Is it capturing what is unique about your company and memorable?

    - 1776: Where Revolutions Begin

A tagline is similar to naming, recommendations are that your tagline be unique, short, different from your competition, and can be protected or trademarked. Typically four words or less is where you should start, keep it simple and easy to say. It is important to look at the name on its own and then with the tagline to have it all be additive. As you create your tagline, make sure you love it and you can also use it when you work with clients. It is a critical element of your personal and company identity. It should reflect the vision of the company and what matters as well as be interesting. Brainstorm ideas and words that you want to consider in your tagline below — including what kind of tagline you want to have. Do you want one that is more imperative or more descriptive? What would fit with your personal brand?

EXERCISE
Developing Your Tagline Ideas

Ideas	Pros / Cons

Colors are Critical to Aligning Your Personal and Company Brand

It is important to recognize the colors you like personally, as well as what you are hoping will represent the company identity too. There is a science behind colors, and they do matter when it comes to creating a connection visually with your customers and prospects. Earlier we talked about choosing key words like bold, energetic, confidence, strength — and these are in fact represented by colors like red and blue. There are some critical questions to ask before you commit to your color(s) and your company color(s).

- One important part of this exercise is to look at what colors competitors are using and understand if color is something that can help you stand out and why they potentially chose those colors.

- Utilizing your key words — look at what colors relate[49] to your key descriptors

- Create your logo in a few colors and see how customers / potential clients feel with those colors

- Remember your target segment, there can be differences in gender preference when it comes to color (although blue is the most popular for both)

- One other consideration is to think about printing, and the complexity of your colors. If you have more than one color, especially three or four, it can be very expensive to get promotional materials printed too.

- You may want to consider colors that are in the same family, or you can create more visual interest with complementary colors (think of colors across from each other on the color wheel).

Here are some additional data points from Column Five[50] when they looked at the top 100 brands (determined by brand value).

- 33% of top brands use blue, 28% use black or grayscale, and 29% use red

- 95% use only one or two colors

- Colors can be warm (energy) or cold (calm and security)

- Warm colors: red, yellow, orange, black

- Cold colors: brown, blue, green, purple

Colors are key to a great first impression. You may want to look at the colors you wear on a regular basis and see if there is synergy between those colors and the colors you envision for your business. Many entrepreneurs leverage the colors that are most authentic to them as well as their audience, it is great to have a win-win.

Designing a Logo You Love, Make It Meaningful

A logo is another very challenging part of the branding process, but it does not have to be excruciating. One of the most critical elements of designing a logo is working to have it represent something about your business, its values, how it makes people feel, or some core concept related to your approach. For BrandMirror, the logo is a representation of perception and reality aligning. A large part of the work I do with clients is understanding "perception is reality" and therefore the more those agree, i.e. your customers see you as you see yourself, then the more powerful you are and the more you can move forward (hence yellow and blue make green). So the more green you have, the more forward progress you can make.

Many entrepreneurs go straight to 99Designs[51] or Fiverr. com[52] to develop a logo and get it done as quickly as possible, partly for efficiency and also cost. Logo design can cost thousands of dollars. However, the more clarity you have on your company's personality, purpose, and intent, the easier it can be to provide guidance should you want to hire 99Designs or Fiverr, or someone else. In my experience, if possible, get a great graphic designer that comes recommended through the Chamber or fellow entrepreneurs, and have a logo created for you that you love. It is important that your logo represents your idea for the company brand and that it resonates with potential customers. Do ask for feedback on the designs and ask customers what the logo makes them think of when they see it. If your logo can convey a story or make it easy for you to explain what you do — great. Your logo is a key part to the beginning part of your journey and being relevant.

In my experience and when working with my clients, here are some tips for designing your logo.

- Remember, you get what you pay for when it comes to design work.

- If you need your business to be professional because you are working with Fortune 500 companies, then pay for a quality logo.

- Get the high quality eps and vector files of your logo from your graphic artist.

- Try not to use stock art, you may want to look at it for ideas, but create something unique like you.

- Find a logo that resonates with your target client, not just you.

- Keep it simple—too much detail makes it hard to print.

- Start with black and white then add color, you want to make sure your logo works in black and white first, that the lack of color does not change the feeling.

- Lastly, find a font that is unique and fits your personality too.

Choosing a Font That Speaks to Your Brand

Think about the classic Coca-Cola script that is recognizable anywhere, or the Disney script that is handwritten out during the previews. These scripts convey meaning and personality. What would your brand look like in a font? Would it be playful, or serious? Would it be strong or creative? Approachable or more classic?

Typically a company will choose one font, and potentially a secondary font that is distinct enough from the first font, yet still adheres to the company personality. Now is a good time to step back and see what you have so far when it comes to developing your brand identity and ensure these elements all align.

Do the colors, logo, and font, align and support the feeling of the company?

There is a great infographic available online, *So You Need a Typeface*[53], that can walk you through the font you might want based on the project you have — book, website, logo, invitation, etc.

One critical factor to keep in mind is how widespread your font is across platforms. Do you use something that was specially created for you or do you need an API to use it? If you are creating documents in PowerPoint, Word, or sending them to customers — do you know that when they open documents everything will work as intended? What about when you go to order materials or SWAG, is your font available or at least a backup one that is very similar? Just ask so you go in eyes wide open. It would be a shame to pay someone to get you a font for your use and then not have it work at your critical customer touchpoints. If there is a font you want to identify, use WhatFont or Fontface Ninja[54], both plugins to explore fonts on a webpage.

Pictures Are Worth a Thousand Words

One of the challenging things when you launch your business and build out your visual brand toolkit is getting photos that look great and yet might be stock photos until you generate enough of your own photos. There are several sites[55] with stunning photos that you could use on your website, card, blogs, etc. Most of these are public domain, but some may need attribution, so just review and make sure you know how to use the images.

- StockSnap.io or Unsplash

- Canva[56] (for creating right sized photos for your social media)

Your photos also convey a personality, so be sure to think about if they are modern, confident, casual, and appropriate or not, before you use them. Especially when it comes to images on websites like social media, LinkedIn, etc. there is a definite blurring between personal and company brand, which is why it is efficient to find photos that work in both spaces.

Once you have your colors, name, font, tagline, logo, and pictures it is definitely time to think about your first website.

Launching Your First Website

There a lot of options for websites, if you are a solopreneur, you could simply use branded.me and pull information from LinkedIn. If you need a website, you could create a site on Weebly.com, Wix.com, or SquareSpace.com. Many people take the time to learn WordPress and create a site, which can be as complex as you want to make it, or relatively simple. The challenge is, it just takes time. Here are some key questions and tips to look at before you start building your site:

- What do you need your website to do? Are you selling products or providing information? Be clear because what you build needs to support that. Find websites you like that you can use as a comparison. Look at competitor sites too.

- Map out with a wireframe app (or on a few sheets of paper) what pages you need, what information goes where, and understand how customers will navigate the site. Keep it simple. Try for 5 or fewer.

- Organize your content ideas and then write draft content — keep it short and highlight the important things to make it easy for customers to find. Not too much text and not too little.

- It is important that your site looks professional, so if you decide to bootstrap it and build it yourself, make sure it looks great. Customers don't care about your website skills, they will care more about how your website looks.

- For your first site, be intentional, but do not overthink it.

- Also, do not overspend on your website for the first one. Look and see what is really needed to get up and running, look professional, and then over the next 6-12 months learn from your customers and you can decide what you need to do to your site looking ahead.

- Own your domain, and potentially others similar to it and redirect them to your site.

- Get a reliable host platform (WordPress, Weebly, Wix, SquareSpace, etc.)

- If you are planning on growing quickly, you may want to have something custom built if you think you will outgrow the "do it yourself" sites.

- Get references if you hire and look at their work. Have they designed comparable sites like yours?

- Be professional, but also personal — have an About Us page

- Always have a contact form and a form to gather emails (e-letter, white paper, etc.) to begin creating email lists

- Have call to actions (complimentary consult, download an e-book, sign up for a webinar, etc.)

- Bring in testimonials and have video where possible

- Make sure you have a responsive site

- Research SEO and at least get the basics

- Test and learn, see how different pages do — set goals for the site and monitor and manage to them.

Your website development budget can be extensive, so be clear on what you need it to do and how it will generate revenue, leads, visibility, etc. Be sure to allocate maintenance time and fees in your resource budget. Sites can go from $500 DIY to $5,000 to $50,000, so get multiple quotes to make sure you are getting the best options based on what you need for the next 1-2 years.

Setting Up Your Email Signature

One easy branding opportunity that creates call to actions, yet goes under leveraged, is using a tool like wisestamp. com to create a nice email signature with your photo, logo, contact info, etc. With wisestamp.com[57] or newoldstamp. com[58] you can include your latest blog, tweet, connect button for LinkedIn and many other social channels. Here is an example of mine:

Jen Dalton *CEO & Founder, BrandMirror*
Mobile: 703-898-8691
jendalton@brandmirror.com | www.brandmirror.com

Let's connect!   Follow on Twitter

Reflections Blog Why Twitter Matters

If you are interested in booking an appointment, please visit my calendly site.
https://calendly.com/jendalton/consultation2015

For a low investment, it can make a great impression, especially when you think about the amount of emails you send on a day to day basis. You can of course create one in Google, but these two tools are much more visually interesting and engaging. Your email signature is a great way to blend your personal and company brands. It is easy to pull in your latest blog while sending people to the company website for a complimentary consult. Think about who will be receiving your emails and be sure you are taking advantage of the capabilities of an email signature. Don't forget the signature on your phone, too.

Getting Your First Business Cards

One of the most exciting things was ordering that first batch of business cards and getting them delivered. Here are a few tips to keep in mind before your order those cards.

- Identify the purpose of the business card — provide your info, marketing, stand out, make an appointment? All of the above?

- Include key info: name, title, numbers, social media, email, address

- Size — some people want a unique size, recommend that it at least fit in a wallet

- Keep it clean and simple, communicate what your business does in an efficient space (include your logo, tagline, -isms)

- When you do build your business card, be sure to use both sides and choose a style and material that sends a clear message about you and the company

- The thicker business card always seems more serious, legit, and committed than the flimsier cards that get lost.

- Also, think about being able to write on the card, vs. having it be too glossy. This makes it easier for someone to take down notes if needed.

- Does the card support your brand? If your company is focused on transparency, would you consider a translucent card?

Think about the values you want to convey through the business card and get creative. Two favorites are Vistaprint[59] and also Moo[60] for ordering business cards. Order a smaller amount and see *how* you use them, then you can always order more as you need them. Both sites also provide printing for flyers, and other things.

Creating Your First Products & Services Online and In Person

When developing your first set of products or services, start by crafting 3 different offerings and try them out on people that are in your client demographic. Below are some illustrative examples to pressure test what you might offer.

- Create one lower price point package (1 hour coaching session for example)

- Develop a middle of the road price point (1/2 day workshop)

- Larger package (1 week, 3 months, etc.)

- Get feedback on the experience, outcome, and pricing. Integrate the feedback as needed and draft your first marketing materials.

Develop your first pass at products and get a sense of who they are for, the price, and how you would describe them to a customer. Brainstorm in the table on the next page.

EXERCISE
Brainstorming Your Product & Services

Product / Service	Description	Client	Cost	Pricing
Ex: 1 hour coaching session	Email w/ assessment, 1 hour phone call, Follow up email w. action items	CEO level	$300 given time and admin	$500

Here are some important marketing materials that leverage and showcase your products:

- Business card

- LinkedIn profile, LinkedIn Company Page

- Swag — like stylus pens (think of items that align with your brand)

- Website, Landing page (if you are not ready for a website)

- First flyer, Postcards, Signage (pop up banners that you can re-use at events)

Your materials should leverage words that resonate with your target clients. Anticipate that your products and services will likely change over time as you learn more about your client needs as well as keep up with and in some cases be ahead of the market.

Leverage the Touchpoint Table to Outline Your Touchpoints

This is where understanding how you and your products & services emotionally resonate is very important. Knowing where your customer is at can help you move them through the process faster. The five stages below are relatively generic. The "Opening the Box" phase is for actual delivery, what that experience is like when they literally or figuratively open the box. You can grab some index cards and tape and map it out on the wall, your desk, etc. to brainstorm what you want to have happen and what it means to the customer. Many companies believe that competition comes down to the best customer experience.

EXERCISE
Defining Your Touchpoint Strategy

Touchpoints / Entry Point	How do they Discover You?	How do they Research choices?	Why do they buy?	Build Value & Loyalty
Where is your customer and what are they doing?				
How can you connect with them emotionally — break the status quo?				
What is holding them back?				
What evidence do you need to convince them?				

CHAPTER 5 SUMMARY

Building Your Reputation One Interaction at a Time

As the founder and first employee, each of the elements in this chapter are grounded in your personal values and beliefs, and have been translated to the company brand where it makes sense. As the face of the company, it is important to leverage these touchpoints strategically. There are other methods like packaging, voicemail, letterhead, signs, newsletters, e-letters, social networks, etc. Some of these we will cover later. The critical next step after this chapter is to look out over the next 6 months and plan out what you need as well as your budget. Some of this can be done with very little budget, but a fair amount will need some investment. Prioritize what you can re-use and re-leverage, like signs. If you make postcards, make them evergreen, avoid putting dates (at least the year) on them if you are simply driving people for a complimentary consult. Every interaction is critical when you are building trust and credibility with your future and current clients.

CHAPTER 6

Develop Evidence Based Branding that Shows & Tells Your Value

"Know yourself. Don't accept your dog's admiration as conclusive evidence that you are wonderful."

ANN LANDERS

One of the most powerful ways to attract clients, investors, and fans is to be *real* with your experiences, provide evidence, and to share your personal stories and be vulnerable. In the last chapter we talked about the icing on the cake (first impression, etc.) — now we are getting to the cake, the important part of your story, in which your evidence showcases why someone wants to work with you. Just like the concept "innocent until proven guilty", people see others as not credible until proven credible.

Now is the time to pull out those experiences and stories that help validate your vision and purpose. Some of my clients are concerned about sharing too much information. You do not have to share everything; this is about being authentic and vulnerable through intentional communication and storytelling. I recommend identifying three to five stories that are authentic and meaningful in so far as they support and convey the importance of your personal and company brand. I always have several key stories that I can pull out and leverage for talks and one on one conversations too. Being prepared does not make them less authentic, it just means I am intentional and ready for any opportunity.

As we work through your stories, it is important to remember that they need substance and soundbites. Whether you are telling your story at a talk or pitching yourself and your idea to a venture capitalist, storytelling matters. Develop your inventory of stories, pieces of evidence, and then practice sharing them with clients to be sure they 1) resonate, 2) are relevant, and 3) help create an emotional connection while building your credibility.

Think about what you can share about your journey that will help build trust with your audience, without sacrificing your security. It is what makes us human that brings us closer and can move us forward. Stories of vulnerability such as when Sheryl Sandberg shared the intimate loss of her husband on Facebook, or when Hillary Clinton shared stories of her mother and what her life was like growing up, are examples of ways to share unique experiences in person, and online, that resonate and meet your audience where they are. It is these stories that bring us together to bring about change and move people forward.

Practicing Your Introduction and Pitch

Whether you are out at events, pitching for funding, or pitching a client, practicing your pitch matters. To sound authentic and credible requires knowing your pitch like the back of your hand and having a few variations so you can off the cuff tweak it based on who you are meeting. Here are a few things you will need to provide for the short pitch (at an event meeting new people):

1. Who are you, and what is your company?

2. Why you and why this company?

3. What is one critical fact/data point that people need to know to understand the pain point you are solving?

4. Can you share a real case study of a client that you helped?

You don't have to present the above information in that order. If you have some extremely compelling data, start with that hook. For example:

Did you know that 55% of the first impression is based on your image? I am committed to making sure that your first impression makes one that gets you business, my name is ..., and my company is..."

Keep it simple and not about you after you make your introduction. I firmly believe that the more interested you are in someone, the more interesting you will be to them.

If you have one minute to pitch, here is a framework to think about leveraging.

EXERCISE
Pitch Pre-Work —
Building Your Persuasive Pitch

What is your purpose?	
Who is your audience?	
What do you know about your purpose that is critical right now?	
What does your audience need to know right now?	
Why do they need to know it?	
Is it relevant to them?	
How does your audience feel about this topic?	
Why isn't change happening now?	
What is your core message or theme?	
How should you organize it? Pain Point / Pitch / Plan? OR Pitch / Pain Point / Plan?	
What evidence do you have to support your point? Data? Quotes? Video? Photos? Materials?	

What is your short introduction?	
What is your conclusion for your audience(s)?	
Do you have a pithy way to summarize it?	

*Leveraged from Prof. Jeanine Turner's Communications Course, Georgetown University with her permission.

Creating Your Bundles of Knowledge, Your Stories that I.M.P.R.E.S.S.

The stories that make an impression highlight your Impact, showcase Metrics, and include Proximity, allow you to describe your Role in an Engaging way, ultimately showing the Scope and Scale of your value and impact. Let's talk through some examples. One of my clients, Jamie, is a serial entrepreneur, who has built an impressive career in financial investing. He has successfully built companies and sold them, and is now working on a portfolio of startups. As a result, he is currently re-positioning his personal brand because many of these new startups are not in markets that he has worked in before now. When we developed his leadership promise, his purpose, we discovered that there was a broader story that showcases why what he is doing now makes even more sense. Jamie is about "enabling and accelerating *the impact of crowd intelligence* by *rewiring* how people come together". So for Jamie, we had to go back and look at his stories to understand what would make an impression and create evidence for his new venture.

To build stories, we needed to look at what is unique about him: innovative, visionary, authentic, heart, humor, creative, ability to translate technology, family, and helping others. Based on his experiences, one of the stories is around how: the internet evolution has had three waves of influence when it comes to financial investments: web/cloud, social/ mobile, and now crowd. Using the I.M.P.R.E.S.S. model provides context for your clients, prospects, and others to "see a picture" a.k.a. story of you and understand what they can do with you and how you can help them.

ILLUSTRATION
Jamie McIntyre, Leveraging the
I.M.P.R.E.S.S. Framework

- *Impact*: Jamie and his extended team developed and built the first asset management platform for High Net Worth Advisory practices (impact is about defining compelling outcomes)

- *Metrics:* Went from a single client to $8 billion in assets under advisement. His platform served over 10X those assets across over 100 firms (metrics are about the numbers — how much revenue, how many people did you manage, how many external teams, how many widgets).

- *Proximity:* Jamie worked with CEOs, was client facing, and worked with developers, advisors, researchers, and entrepreneurs (proximity tells your audience who you interacted with on a regular basis so they have context on where to place you in their narrative. Saying you worked with CEOs and developers is very different than simply saying you worked with a cross-functional team)

- *Role:* Jamie co-founded this company and brought together people to develop a solution that was purchased by another firm for use (describing your role matters because sometimes titles just do not tell your audience enough, this can also include sharing what your company did because sometimes that is also not well known)

- *Engaging:* Jamie focuses on providing technology solutions with empathy (write your content in a way that is engaging)

- *Scope & Scale:* Grew the solution, and company. Leveraging these insights to continue to speak nationally on how to integrate technology into high touch client relationships where listening and empathy are still critical. (show your impact)

Creating evidence means you are bringing information to bear and validating, shifting, or updating people's perceptions of where you are at and what you can do. One of our first efforts on updating his personal brand was to plan out what new evidence should be delivered to bring his audience with him on the journey. We started with updating his talks, blogs, and slowly "dripping" out more of his insights and perspectives on the intersection of people and technology and what that looks like for the future. Not only did the evidence support his external persona, the process encouraged him to embrace his values and build an app[61], www.heartstringsapp.com, that helps people share their own stories and appreciation for each other. What story, or stories, do you have that would build the credibility of your capabilities?

EXERCISE
Leveraging the I.M.P.R.E.S.S. Framework

High Level Story	
Impact: what impact did you have?	
Metrics: how can you use information and data to show your impact?	
Proximity: paint a picture of the level of people and what people you worked with in the past, or currently	
Role: what do you do?	
Engaging: be interesting, not boring	
Scope: what is your scope of work?	
Scale: what is the scale of your impact over time?	

Creating Evidence is About Being Intentional and Planning Ahead

You may be wondering what evidence looks like. Here is a great way to see if you have any valid, useful evidence. Examine your LinkedIn profile. What evidence do you see that either shows or tells of your value and impact? Here are *some examples of evidence*:

- Stories with metrics — what results did you deliver?

- Photos in action (coaching a client, in your store, doing volunteer work)

- A video of you introducing yourself or delivering a short list of insights

- A presentation you gave at a conference (simplified if you need to remove confidential content), upload it on Slideshare

- A call to action for people to come to your next event

- Recommendations/Testimonials

- A link to your blog, an article you wrote, an interview, etc.

- Awards nominated for or received

- Social media participation and content is evidence of your brand

- Deliver talks and highlight topics with a photo (Speaker Reel video)

- Leading or participating in a webinar and podcast

- Leveraging Blab, a live discussion site, which also allows for invite only

- Use the live video sharing app, Periscope, which had 1 million users its first day (it is like a behind the scenes kind of tool)

- Vine for creating short videos

Whether it is your LinkedIn page, your website, your business card — every touchpoint plays a role in making an impression and working for you while you are out running your business. Generating evidence is a habit, build it into your marketing plan — remind yourself to take pictures of you along with others at events, tweet live, or post on Facebook the next day about whatever you did that is relevant to your audience. Another reason evidence matters is that it shows your clients and prospects how you act, interact, make decisions, and think. It gives them a window in to you and what your values are, how you show up, and how you can help them. One of my posts, "The 5 Mistakes You Are Making on LinkedIn"[62], generated over 60K views on LinkedIn, over 45 consults, which turned into revenue.

ILLUSTRATION
How Blogging / Posting on LinkedIn Can Get You Visibility & Impact

Jennifer (Jen) Dalton
CEO | Thought Leadership & Master Brand
Strategist | Be a Noisebreaker, Not a Noisemaker .

5 Mistakes You are Making on LinkedIn

Feb 8, 2015 | 64,825 views   335 Likes   136 Comments

When I work with clients there are dozens of things we cover when it comes to LinkedIn. However, there are 5 opportunities that I wanted to highlight that seem to be common gaps from CEOs to college students.

Your Evidence Comes from Your Areas of Expertise

You may have noticed that frameworks and visuals are a big part of how I work with my clients. One of my clients has had her business for years and needed guidance on what evidence would help her be more visible and relevant to her clients. Jo Ann Skinner has an amazing business, Opening Doors to Growth[63], that started from her personal experiences with ADHD (attention deficit/hyperactive disorder). Although her background is in corporate America as a vice president, her focus shifted to starting her own business after working with individuals in her family and beyond dealing with the challenges of ADHD. Millions of people struggle with some level of ADHD, and Jo Ann has built a business through training, certifications, and personal experience to help others cope. One of the big pieces of evidence is that she is a credentialed coach through ICF, a Certified ADHD Coach, and also a Board Certified Coach. When we worked together, we identified very specific customers and then focused on developing a content strategy. We mapped Jo Ann's three main Areas of Expertise in the three circles. Then we began to use those to outline and brainstorm sub-topics that would matter to her audiences. You can see where we call out helping college students, other ADHD coaches, and executives. The exercise below helped Jo Ann decide where to spend her time. Since then she has already written her first blog within a week of working together.

The Venn diagram approach provides a way to look at your focus areas and identify where capabilities intersect and how you can create interesting topics from them. The framework blends Jo Ann's expertise across her company (which is all about providing systematic solutions and strategies for those with ADHD), her skills (which are executive coaching, ADHD), and her passion (entrepreneurship from her business background). As the CEO, you can bring multiple facets of your identity into your story and make it very interesting and engaging.

ILLUSTRATION
Reputation Rings — Jo Ann's Areas of Expertise & Focus

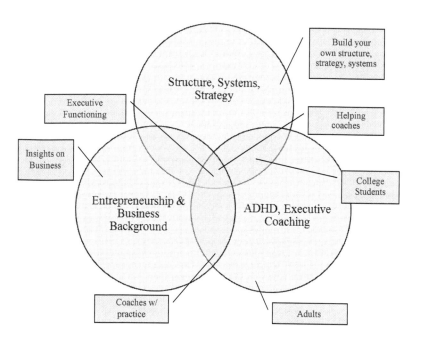

Another critical part of the evidence is creating your frameworks and structures for your business. For example, Jo Ann coaches her clients on developing their systems to work more effectively, learn better, and stay focused — from college students to executives. Although she had a system she used, it was not named, mapped, or codified.

Develop Your Intellectual Property and Methods of Delivering Value

Think about it, when you go to work with someone, would you rather see the process for how they work or just have a handshake and a promise that it will happen? The bigger the dollar value, the more likely you want to see evidence of how someone works and what they do along the way. Developing your frameworks and methods is helpful for you to run more consistently, follow your process, and show clients you know what you are doing. Plus you can protect your ideas, frameworks, designs. One of the first structures we built for Jo Ann codified her approach to working with clients. She is good at helping other people, and she is very busy and had not taken a moment to codify her steps. Once we started mapping the steps, it was very easy for her to articulate them. A key question was how to fit the structure within her current brand: logo, colors, visuals, wording, etc. Her logo is comprised of five leaves in it to symbolize growth; consequently we developed a five step process that aligns with her logo. It sounds simple, yet isn't that usually the best outcome? Keep it simple. In Chapter 8 we will discuss how you protect your ideas and frameworks.

A Blog is a Great, and Cost Effective Way, to Build Your Reputation

I am sure you have heard people suggest you write a blog to build your visibility. It is absolutely a fantastic way to show how you think and share your expertise. I remember when I first sat down to write a blog, the blank document on my screen was so painful. It is critical to concentrate only on your areas of expertise and brainstorm interesting blog topics and perspectives. At a talk I gave in London in 2014 at the User Experience Association, one person asked what they should blog about during my talk. I asked them what they were good at in their job and passionate at outside of work: UX design and the Tango. Wouldn't it be different to read a blog about *five ways the tango inspired my UX design*?

Here are ingredients that work for me when writing a blog:

ILLUSTRATION
BrandMirror — DNA of an Engaging Blog

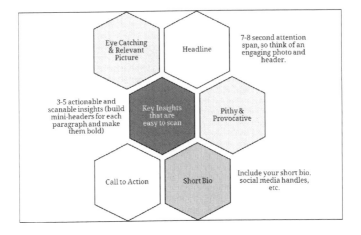

People forget 90% of what they read or see within a week[64] — so what is your 10% message? As you write your blog, think of the one headline, or one liner, you want them to take away. Then simply identify three critical points that support your one liner. It helps to brainstorm and share your thoughts with others to get input and feedback.

If You Have Their Attention, They Can Remember Your Message

1. Use Visuals to Get Their Attention

2. Use Graphics to Convey Information

3. Use Share-worthy Soundbites to Get Their Attention

4. Keep It Easy to Scan (read quickly) and Share

Given how mobile people are, they are typically scrolling and scanning on their phone, it is important to have a high "scan-ability" or "scroll-ability" factor. I literally mean make it easy to read quickly.

First, get a picture that gets your audience's attention. We use real photos where possible, Canva, and other sites, to have genuine images. Develop a title that is a hook — top mistakes, top questions, or a creative one like the tango example. Then you can build your blog out like the example below.

- **TITLE**

- Intro paragraph (3–5 sentences)

- **Mini-headline, 1st key point (bold)**

- 1–2 paragraphs

- **Mini-headline, 2nd key point (bold)**

- 1–2 paragraphs

- **Mini-headline, 3rd key point (bold)**

- 1–2 paragraphs

- *We recommend 3–5 paragraphs, but no more without risk of losing the reader's attention.

- Closing paragraph (do you have a call to action? Book to read, reach out to you, share if you like, etc.)

- Your sign off (Sincerely, your name)

- Your Bio (3–5 sentences, link to website, email, etc.)

Other evidence to consider in your blog, you may want to insert a video from YouTube, or a link to an article. Maybe even a podcast. Think of the resources you have available to make this shareable. A Slideshare[65] would be a great thing to embed.

CHAPTER 6 SUMMARY

Be Intentional and have Fun Building Evidence

Just as you focus on your customers and clients, it is important to take time and invest in your thought leadership and develop your content and evidence. You can leverage evidence to demonstrate your value and connect with people. Whether you are meeting people in person or sharing content online, evidence of how you think, what you do, the impact you have made is critical to shaping your audience's perception in a positive way. It is imperative to create your evidence on a regular basis. This chapter shared examples of key ways to think about delivering evidence with your pitch/introduction, tactical evidence like photos, videos, and blogging. It is critical to review your evidence on a regular basis and ensure that you have the right evidence to showcase your value and expertise. Every year you should think about the business goals you have and then back into what evidence you would need to make those goals easier to hit. For example, if you want to add speaking to your offerings, and get paid thousands of dollars, how do you show you are worth that amount of money? By developing your strength as a speaker. A speaker reel demonstrating how great you are as a speaker is one way to build targeted evidence that supports your brand and reputation.

EXERCISE
Build Your Evidence Inventory — What topics could you talk or write about now?

Topic	Headline	3–5 points	Evidence	Call to Action
Ex: Small Businesses Can Go Green	Top 5 Ways to Save Time & Money in Your Office	Map your process Evernote Scheduling Tools Pens that write to your laptop Top Apps	Image of Clutter — before and after? Top insights from organizers	Call for a complimentary consult, attend a webinar, etc.

CHAPTER 7

Conceptualize Your CEO Reputation Strategy

> "Absorb what is useful, reject what is useless, add what is specifically your own."
>
> **BRUCE LEE**

Every entrepreneur faces the dilemma of time management. In most cases the question of how much time to invest in the CEO reputation never comes up, comes up sort of haphazardly, or very intentionally for CEOs who have a strong reputation. Because the CEO, and especially the solopreneur, has so little time available, the "squeaky wheel" gets the oil. The squeaky wheel is typically profitability, employee issues, customer management, business development, crises, etc. The irony is that with an intentional reputation strategy, many of these issues can be mitigated, solved, or completely avoided all together. The focus of this chapter is to help you articulate what you conceptually need to do with your reputation as it relates to your business, and clearly understand how that looks strategically and tactically.

It is important to start with the end in mind when it comes to designing what you will need to build. One critical question is: what can your reputation do? Articulate what outcomes you want and need your reputation to deliver on for you and your business. Early on in the book, we discussed the buckets for you to consider when it comes to your reputation: company awareness, business development, client relations, employee relations, and thought leadership. It includes understanding to what extent does your reputation support the business goals, provide return on investment, aid in your time management, promote your visibility, and enable you to delegate, be transparent, and learn new things. When you look in the mirror, who do others see and who do you see?

Leveraging Your Reputation Intentionally

When you think about reputation strategy and determining where you want to position yourself and how you want to show up, there is definitely a way to ease into being more visible and digitally social. You do not have to start off doing five tweets a day and video blogging. In fact, you should not start doing anything until you've thought about your personal and company goals. The *Reputation Relevance Continuum* below can be a starting place to identify where you want to invest your time and resources. Which of those boxes speak to a need or gap you see in your own reputation? Are you simply there, or powerfully engaged? How are you increasing the company's relevance from reactive to proactive leadership?

ILLUSTRATION
Reputation Relevance Continuum

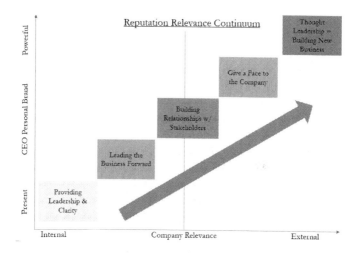

Reputation Relevance Continuum

Where do you want to focus on the continuum? What matters to your business goals next year and beyond? As you do continuous strategic planning, integrating the CEO reputation as a lever to pull is critical.

EXERCISE
Identify the Top Goals Your Reputation Can Deliver on for the Company

Top Business Goals for Next 12 Months	What Can You Do as CEO to Help?
Example: 3 new strategic partnerships	*Attend targeted events to meet and grow prospects*
1.	
2.	
3.	
4.	
5.	

Leveraging Your Reputation to Increase Relevance

One of the most critical reputation drivers (Weber Shandwick, 2015) for a CEO is the ability to provide a vision to the employees and key constituents. As you look at how present you are in each interaction, are you building a strong reputation as a visionary leader? What opportunities do you have? Here are some of the top drivers of a strong CEO reputation according to the Weber Shandwick report, *The CEO Reputation Premium*[66].

- Has a clear vision for the company

- Inspires & motivates others

- Is honest and ethical

- Is a good communicator internally

- Cares that the company is a good place to work at

- Has a global business outlook (broader viewpoint)

- Is a good communicator externally

- Is decisive

- Is focused on customers

Every CEO has an opportunity to show up as a visionary leader, and someone that cares about their employees and customers. One of the most compelling reasons to build your reputation and visibility as a CEO is tied to attracting and managing your talent. Leveraging your values to help your company stand out as compelling and a great place to work can definitely help you "win the war" on talent.

Great Leaders with Great Values Attracts Great Talent

As the CEO, it is important to understand how your vision and values influence your company culture and talent. A regional construction company in Virginia, Exterior Medics[67], is focused on "delivering exceptional customer service while installing industry leading products by expert craftsman." When I interviewed one of the founders, Mark Watson, I asked him how hiring played into their reputation and success formula. He answered "to accomplish this goal we need exceptional people, anything less just won't do." From finding, training, keeping, and inspiring their employees, Mark and his business partner Joe clearly live their values and beliefs.

Mark and Joe have always believed in "hiring on personality and training the skill, no matter the position." That's not to say that they throw all other credentials out of the window, but if the candidate does not project a positive energy and enthusiasm for the position, they aren't too interested in what a candidate has done. The skills that it takes to do any particular job, though they may come easier to some more than others, are not necessarily natural to anyone, so there isn't an overwhelming emphasis on the skills. Attitude, enthusiasm, optimism, and energy are not as easy to teach.

Sure, Mark and Joe focus on providing motivation, but if an individual doesn't naturally possess these attributes they find they are starting off on the wrong foot. Needless to say, they've found that the best looking resume does not always translate into the best employee.

The message they deliver to every potential team member they interview is always the same: "You have the opportunity to make a difference here." They are a close knit family-style business that cares as much for their employees as they do for their clients. They believe that if you help the company fulfill its commitment to exceptional service for their clients, you'll have a lot of fun. Mark and Joe celebrate and reward team members with performance bonuses, employee appreciation days, catered breakfasts, extra days off, a holiday party, etc. As they grow as a company, they are committed to never losing focus on ensuring that each member of the team is growing with them. It is much easier to find a great customer than it is to find a great employee. In their mind, outstanding employees will make getting customers much easier.

Recently they conducted a week-long training program for their sales team with the goal to sharpen their skill set. The first two days of this training were focused entirely on optimism, enthusiasm, and energy. It's their belief that without an optimistic outlook, coupled with an abundance of enthusiasm and energy for what you do, an individual cannot possibly be at their best for the client they are meant to serve. As a company, they are excited for every opportunity to assist a client with their specific wants and needs, it's vital that their Sales Team delivers this message not through showing how much they know, but by showing how much they care. They are extremely focused on being the best at every trade and service that they offer through ongoing training programs, both onsite and offsite.

Mark and Joe always had the vision that Exterior Medics would be much more than just another construction company. Of course, they understand that above all else they have to deliver the best project to each and every client. Beyond that, they want to be thought of as a trusted advisor and resource to their clients and the rest of the community. To showcase their commitment to the community, they launched their magazine, *House Calls*. It is a great example of how they are trying to achieve influence and how their community perceives them. House Calls was created to promote not only the work Exterior Medics is doing on individual homes, but more importantly the work that they are doing to give back and provide additional value. Every issue of House Calls features a charity that they are affiliated with (these charities are brought to them by employees), DIY tips for homeowners, "self-help" tips from various sources, local community events, other local small businesses.

In this example, Mark and Joe have woven their values into their company and are making sure they find the right talent and then continually invest in that talent. When talking to one of their employees, Steve Harper, he said he had never worked at a place where people were so happy. Remember that your employees are an extension of your brand, your values, and your vision. Bringing them on the journey with you as a leader; helping them feel vested in the team and part of something bigger are key to building your reputation as a leader. Happy employees will definitely help make happy customers.

What Return is there on Reputation? Can I Measure ROR?

As any good business owner, you are asking what the return is on managing your reputation and the amount of time, money, and other resources you put into it. One critical element of managing your reputation is consistency. Think of it as bringing your brand to life, giving it a heartbeat, a pulse. How many times do you think you need to be visible based on your business goals? Below is an illustrative Visibility Calendar to give you an example of what CEO engagement might be for next year. The examples listed in the table are simply meant to reflect an intentional way to plan on being present, submitting content, speaking with target audiences. The table is illustrative. However, the main takeaway is simply to be intentional and think of your reputation as a tool in your toolkit that creates value for the business. Map out a month to month plan with your staff and marketing team how you want to integrate into the broader marketing and editorial calendar.

ILLUSTRATION
CEO Visibility Calendar, Ideas for Being Visible

Focus Areas	• This is a Quarterly View, Recommend Monthly
Business Milestones	• Ad Hoc Wins • Company Anniversary • Holiday Party
Drive Awareness	• Awards Submission for CEO / Company ABC Award • Community Event
Business Development	• Weekly / Monthly Networking Event • Attend Speak @XYZ Conference
Client Relations	• Quarterly Client Check In — Phone Call / Email • Thank You Event for Clients Together, w/ Speaker
Employee Relations	• Strategic Planning • Monthly All Hands • Weekly Leadership Team Meeting • Team Building • Skip Levels • Recognition Lunch • Lunch N' Listen
Thought Leadership	• Monthly Video • Weekly or Monthly Blogs

ILLUSTRATION
Jill Erber, Owner of Cheesetique

I first met Jill over a year ago at a Vistage event and was thrilled to learn that she has a restaurant business focused on cheese and wine, Cheesetique[68]. Although her business initially started in 2004 as a small cheese shop, over time, and based on customer demand, it grew to a restaurant with a full menu. Then she opened her second location a few years ago and is on to her third location in 2016. What originally started as a lifestyle business, when Jill left her corporate job to start a family, soon became an opportunity for spreading the word about cheese while providing financial benefits. Talking with Jill you get to know someone who is committed to building a sustainable and scalable business. Someone who is genuinely interested in the numbers as much as she is the specialty cheese.

As a business owner it is critical to understand the mechanics of the health and wealth of your business. Jill has done such a fabulous job building a team of over 80 people, that it allows her to work on the business, not be trapped in it. One of the most important things Jill did was to develop the "Curd Values" — which allowed her to hire based on character and personality and then train people the needed skills. This helped ensure her employees live the brand day to day. Although Jill typically promotes from within the team, when she sought her Director of Operations, she went externally given the expansion to three stores. Identify what you can delegate to help you work on the business more and leverage your time to build the business and grow.

Jill has built a reputation for being bold, approachable, and fun. The feelings that relate to those descriptors show up in the logo design, the colors, and even the environment of the restaurant. Everyone is welcome and their employees are supposed to welcome customers "as if seeing them is the best thing that happened to them all day."

For Jill, like most entrepreneurs, time is critical. When looking at Jill's business goals over the coming year, it really focuses on getting additional visibility through media, continuing to be financially sound during expansion, and finding a great mentor in the restaurant area.

Jill and I discussed her content strategy and what to focus on given her "Reputation Rings", i.e. her three areas of expertise. She has built up knowledge as a restauranteur, a mom that left corporate to start a company, and someone truly passionate about business performance. As she looks ahead to outline the return on her reputation — she can focus on speaking more and potentially doing podcasts or interviews. She could identify events and conferences where she might find a mentor, or simply look on LinkedIn and reach out. She could also blog or do additional videos to highlight insights and best practices from her business. Being big on helping other entrepreneurs, Jill launched AWE, Alexandria Women Entrepreneurs in 2014, which has 15 members that meet monthly focused on peer to peer mentorship. This is a great example of a way to get visibility and build your business connections too.

Hypothetically, if she chose to do 12 things, that is one a month. She could do four things in each of her goal buckets and map out the year intentionally. Once she takes a stab at drafting that plan, then she can look at real metrics and the return on investment and make a more informed decision on where to spend her time. Brainstorming with a starting point at least keeps one moving forward and ensuring investments are aligned to the business goals and needs.

Where to Invest My Time as CEO: Four Ways to Get Started

The above calendar may have made your heart beat faster and, if it did, then pick one thing you want to do differently and better next month — you do not need to do everything listed above starting right now. Then add another one the following month. You can look over the past 12 months and recognize what you want to keep, start, stop, or change when it comes to your reputation. The right answer is different for each CEO, and not everyone will need the same strategy. Think about what you do now and where you could do it better, then add in something each week or month by blocking time on your calendar to do it. If you do not block time on your calendar, it will likely not happen. We are not talking about an unreasonable time commitment. Here are examples of *four easy ways that my clients have gotten started, to a reasonable, practical extent:*

- *Be Efficient and Re-Purpose Content:* One blog a month on LinkedIn, written as a post, and re-leveraged on their company website (it creates other content for customer emails, social media, etc.).

- *Business Development:* Connect with two new people on LinkedIn each week (this might take 5–10 minutes at most a week). Attend two networking events a month.

- *Video Development:* Look at the year and think about what videos you likely will need. If possible film them ahead of time, in one sitting. Then use them as you need them.

- *Develop a Marketing Calendar:* Simply map out key initiatives and goals each month for the year and flag where you can be proactive and plan your own visibility and block your calendar.

For each of the above you can develop a cost, because it is your time. You can also set goals for each one such as: number of views, comments, responses to your blog if you had a Call to Action like complimentary consult, new business leads, new deals, new followers on social media, etc. Measure what you want to manage and hold yourself and your team accountable for tracking results.

One thing that is critical, if you do take action, is to make sure it is doing something you love. If you hate writing, then writing a blog may not work for you. If you love speaking, then invest in that. Implement one or more actions that you are most likely to accomplish in order to initially build momentum and consistency. Quick wins matter.

Who Can I Delegate This to on My Team or Outside of My Team?

There is likely no way to delegate all of it. You want to provide direction and likely review materials at some cadence. For example, when one of my clients asked me to manage their social media (content and posting), we developed an interaction / operating agreement. We would develop content by Thursday, they would review it Friday — make edits, then we would schedule one week at a time. It was anchored on a broader annual calendar to stay ahead of bigger events, but the day to day social media was approved weekly. We leveraged Google Drive and Buffer[69] at the time. Google Drive was excellent to share documents and be able to co-edit and co-create content without emailing back and forth. Buffer was useful as a scheduling tool and provided solid reporting on engagement and top posts.

If you do delegate externally, be sure to compare vendors to whom you delegate and ask if they have worked for similar companies, industries, etc. Either way, know that ramping up will take some time initially before it saves you time. If you decide to keep your content in-house with your team, or even with an intern, develop the same cadence that works for you and your team for managing content and staying ahead of the material as much as possible. Weave in your reputation into the strategy planning, monthly check-ins, etc.

If you are doing this on a small budget, think about ways to get others to research for you — such as on Fiverr[70]. Maybe you want to get some research done on Fiverr; hire several people at a low cost, sift through multiple people's works and pull out the best quality content. You could also speak with career centers at local universities or your alma mater and look at hiring interns to help too. Another option is to hire professionals who are at different points in their life through sites like FlexJobs[71] or Corps Team, previously known as MomCorps[72]. Whatever effort needs to be put in to building your reputation, there is a way to find people, budget, resources, or time to move forward, though you might need to be creative about it. If possible, get help from someone, especially if this is not your strength. Many entrepreneurs barter and trade services if needed as well, especially when just starting out.

Be Transparent, Ask for Help & Visibility if You Have Opportunities to Learn

Look at your network, your current relationships, and identify people who are already good at what you want to do — write, speak, do videos, etc. Sit down with them and ask them to mentor you, or share insights. If you identify that you need to pay someone to coach you on speaking, consider that an investment that should also have a return on value too. When I first started focusing my business on personal branding, I looked into certifications and training. Every year I get re-certified and stay current on the latest thinking and trends. In addition, I reach out and leverage my network to help me. I am already excited about 2016 because I will be investing in my speaking skills even more

— although I have very positive feedback as a speaker — it is always great to talk to experts and keep learning.

No one is telepathic, so make sure you communicate what you want and what you are thinking with your team, partners, and network when it comes to your reputation building efforts. Let people you trust know what you are working on and how you want to support the business. Most people are happy to help you gain more visibility with introductions, doing interviews, panels, etc.

If you need to work on your speaking ability, which most people fear as much as they fear death and taxes, then make getting a speaking coach a priority. Investing in your development to make you a better leader is very important when you think about staying relevant. Even if you think you are a great speaker, do a coaching session at least once and see how it helps.

There are many CEO peer groups which can provide coaching and value from leaders at your same level. Identify groups that would make a great fit, ones you can learn from that push you. It is important to have the support networks to help you be more vulnerable and gain more understanding of your reputation as CEO and how to leverage it. Being CEO is a lonely role, so look into networking groups like Vistage[73], YPO[74], EO[75], and others, to see which communities fit your budget and need.

You Will Need to Learn and Evolve as a CEO to be Relevant

One thing is definitely true — as CEO you will always be evolving and learning. Whether it is something like how to Tweet, give talks, or become more motivational — embrace new skills and insights as much as you can even though it is hard. Your employees, clients, and other constituents will see that and grow to think more of you. If you look at the top Fortune 500 CEOs, according to Weber Shandwick, The Social CEO Report, 68% of them are not social, as in not on social media. However, if you look at the Fortune 500 CEOs under the age of 42, they all have at least one social media account (KPC, 2014). As the CEO, it is critical to be able to find your stakeholders where they are, even if that means learning how to be more social media savvy. You have many people to help. If most conversations are online, capitalize on that and don't be the last one to join. By then it will be too late.

CHAPTER 7 SUMMARY

Identify Your Opportunities for Big Return and Go for It

Even if you decide not to be the one on social media, at least be intentional about declaring where you alternatively want to invest your resources and how to position yourself to create value for the company, its clients, employees, and the community. Looking ahead at your business goals, what ideas come to mind? Write them below, so you do not forget. Below is just for one month. You should plan this out for 6–12 months.

EXERCISE
Develop Your CEO Visibility Calendar

Focus Areas	What would you do to be more visible each month?
Milestones	
Drive Awareness	
Business Development	
Client Relations	
Employee Relations	
Thought Leadership	

Building your brand does not have to cost a fortune, however doing nothing will absolutely cost you business. Many clients say that they have tons of word of mouth business, and ask, why do they need to do invest in their reputation and visibility? The reality is that you could be doing well, however why not do better? If you are not building your reputation and attracting talent and customers, someone else is. Investing in your reputation is no longer optional.

CHAPTER 8

Protect Your CEO Brand Proactively & Reactively

> "It takes 20 years to build a reputation and five minutes to ruin it. If you think about that, you'll do things differently."
>
> **WARREN BUFFETT**

We all remember the BP oil spill in the Gulf. When BP's former CEO Tony Hayward responded to a reporter about the Deepwater Horizon oil spill, the words he uttered were heard around the world: "There's no one who wants this thing over more than I do, I'd like my life back." Later he resigned. In less than a minute he had tarnished his brand as an empathetic leader and problem solver. He clearly did not think about the consequences before he spoke those words.

Before we jump into building your tactical plan for engaging online and in person, let's talk about what you have in place to protect your reputation first. It is vital to think about what protocols, rules, and guidelines you have in place on how to engage if there is a crisis, or manage negative reviews online, reports in the media, etc. Also, you should have protocols for what to do when there is good news too. Protecting your brand means more than just online reviews. It also means protecting your intellectual property, being clear on policies in your industry (especially if it is regulated) on what you can and cannot say or do, and even having regular drills every quarter so your team knows how to respond if there is a crisis.

Always Pause and Think Before You Respond

This seems like such a simple concept, to take a moment, pause, and think before you answer a media question, a Facebook post, a Tweet, a question at a conference. However, there are many examples where in the heat of the moment, or if the CEO was tired, or having an off day, he or she simply said something without thinking. Here are some examples[76] that are worth reviewing. These could potentially have been avoided if they thought about how the words would sound to their audience.

- When Lululemon founder Chip Wilson was forced to apologize for basically calling a segment of his customers overweight by saying "some women's bodies just don't actually work" for the $100 yoga pants. He resigned, and the stock plunged too.

- Mike Jefferies made a similar comment when he was CEO of Abercrombie & Fitch; he stated he wanted his company to market to "cool, good-looking people" and then basically admitted later that his store was exclusionary — resulting in lots of their clothes being donated by young people to shelters.

On a positive note, let's say you discover you have great news, you won an award, or had great customer feedback, or just got quoted in an article. The same logic applies: sit down, plan out how you can leverage it quickly and powerfully. Or, you may want to wait to use it in some more intentional way.

There could be unforeseen events where you need to react quickly because the response window for a great opportunity is a short one. One example that stands out was in 2015 when there was a blackout at the Super Bowl and Oreo sent their infamous tweet: "Power out? No Problem" and the photo with an Oreo and the phrase: "You can still dunk in the dark". With over 15K retweets and 6K likes, that was great visibility for the company that was free. So when things are happening real time, be ready to take action, but just pause briefly and ensure that what you are doing will not cause a backlash.

Responding to Crisis Effectively is Key to Protecting the CEO & Company Brand

As the CEO, you are working to build the brand of your company every day. Unfortunately, in a very short time frame a crisis can hit and upend everything. If your firm has a crisis, one of the most powerful roles of the CEO is to be the face of the organization and lead it forward while being the empathetic, contrite (if appropriate) voice to the public. In many cases, the CEO is the first to be able to respond quickly, followed by the communications and PR team. For CEOs, this is where being on social media can be powerful, provided you have built a following along the way. You do not want to get online the day you have a crisis. The reality is that the public expects to get information quickly and honestly.

As the CEO, it is important to work with your leadership and communications teams to quickly respond and draft your 100 Day plan. Here are some important things to consider:

- Stay calm and cool — do not react out of anger or frustration

- Share the facts you have; however, be cautious not to over share internal information

- Work to fix the issue immediately

- Maintain ongoing visibility and communication when it makes sense

One example of a quick response was when Tony Fernandes, CEO of AirAsia, posted on Twitter, "I as your group ceo will be there through these hard times. We will go through this terrible ordeal together and I will try to see as many of you," within hours of the disappearance of Flight 8501 with 162 people on board. Within 12 hours, he had shared a dozen tweets and they in turn were retweeted thousands of times. The company's official social media account responded as well, posting regular updates to Twitter and Facebook.

In contrast, look at how Malaysia Airlines handled Flight 370 when it disappeared. Many passenger families were given very little information and families were extremely upset with Malaysia Airlines.

Southwest Airlines shared information via Twitter and Facebook regarding an accident very quickly and promised more information soon regarding the flight 345 in 2013. Their quick response highlighted the need to have a plan and procedure in place with scripts and clear roles ready for various scenarios.

The Red Cross had a case where social media caused the issue. You may remember in 2011 when their employee accidentally tweeted something meant for their personal account on the corporate account. The tweet was deleted immediately, and the American Red Cross tweeted that "We've deleted the rogue tweet but rest assured the Red Cross is sober, and we've confiscated the keys." This is a great example where deleting the tweet made sense because they acknowledged the tweet immediately and used humor to explain what happened mitigating a much larger potential PR crisis. The Red Cross wrote a follow up blog and leveraged it as a way to engage, and the employee also apologized from their personal Twitter account — all with humility and humor. If you make a mistake, just own up and fix it.

When it comes to responding online, be very aware of the power of social media. One silly or unintentional comment can snowball quickly. Constantly have someone monitoring and ready to engage quickly, reducing the chances of things getting out of control.

Define Your Role as CEO in the Customer Recovery Process

You will get customer complaints at some point, so have a policy, process, training, and a plan for how to handle them. For you and also for your team, it is important to have "alerts" and monitoring happening (Google Alerts on your name, the company name, leadership team members) and be ready to engage. Here are a few tips when responding to a complaint overall:

- Listen and let them know you understand their complaint

- Don't take it personally and apologize quickly and sincerely

- Stay positive and work to solve the issue — make the customer complete

- Don't highlight what went wrong, go to the customer with a few options to choose from to solve the problem — it can make solving the issue go faster

- See if there are patterns overall and implement improvements

Great companies empower employees to deliver outstanding recovery options. Again, develop this early on and review it on a regular basis. Remember, they are giving you a chance to fix it — which is powerful, you want them to shout out how outstanding you were in the recovery process, not tell everyone the bad news of how you made a mistake and recovered horribly. As the face of the company, that may mean that you are the one to make it right, especially as a solopreneur, or if it is a high value customer they may even expect a call or visit from you.

Develop Policies or Guidelines for Your Company for Using Social Media

One of the easiest suggestions is to create a social media policy or guideline for your company. You will want to guide your employees on what is appropriate and not allowed. Keep in mind that you want to be very careful about what you tell employees they can or cannot do on their personal social media sites. The National Labor Relations Board released a report[77] in 2011 detailing the outcomes of 14 cases involving employer's social and general media guidelines. Here are some best practices.

- Adidas®: use disclaimers that you are not speaking for the company[78]

- Adidas®: you are responsible for what you post; review it with your manager if you are not sure

- Best Buy®: not allowed to share client information, customer information, financial, legal, or operational information

- HP has a Blogging Code of Conduct [79] that states the company's right to review, delete, and correct blogs.

- Be sure to remind your employees about copyright laws given the ease of media online

- Remind employees not to engage in rude behavior

- Provide social media training for your employees, up to and including the CEO

A best practice suggested by Social Media Examiner[80] is to "bring together a broader team and develop your policy and guideline as a group." It would be good to include compliance, or your business attorney, for example. They suggest having "a policy for social media on the job versus social media in their personal lives."

As the CEO, be mindful that your presence online should be very strategic and adhere to policies for social media. Partnering with your marketing and legal teams to plan the right information at the right time is very important. As CEO, you will be under scrutiny.

Highly Regulated Industries Should Still be on Social Media, Just Carefully

One of the first places we go for information is online. However, there are many industries that cannot engage online such as financial services, law, insurance, alcohol and tobacco, industries that serve government entities, and pharmaceuticals, partly because the regulators have struggled with how to develop guidelines and policies. For example, if someone "likes" a wealth management firm on Facebook, is that considered a testimonial? Or simple things like how to include a disclaimer in 140 characters on Twitter? Don't lose hope if you are in a highly regulated industry, especially as a sole practitioner. Keep these tips in mind for your industry.

- Know what regulations apply (HIPAA for health care, SEC for financial institutions, for example) and build a process with accountabilities for who owns the posts, so it is contained as much as possible

- There are guidelines for each channel — and also if you are doing paid activities (in your review make sure posts are compliant)

- Set clear goals and keep it simple and realistic, given the rules, what makes sense for how much time you want to invest and what your customers need

- You can still listen to feedback and monitor topics, etc. to influence your improvement agenda

- Set guidelines on what not to post as well and make sure you review marketing posts and your guidelines on a regular basis in case they need updating

- Archive your social media conversations with tools like ArchiveSocial and Smarsh

- Be consistently present if you need to outsource your social media work

One of my previously mentioned clients, Judy Redpath, founder of Vista Wealth Strategies, is in the wealth management business. The financial services industry (along with others) has very specific rules regarding testimonials, recommendations, etc. and what you can post on social media, say, and share. Much of this is because the industry is highly regulated and people can consider what is said or posted "advice." Even on LinkedIn, skills cannot be endorsed — they must be turned off, disabled. Recommendations are not allowed either since they are all viewed as endorsements. Even when she does want to share content, everything has to be approved in advance. Here are some thoughts on what can be done to protect yourself while getting value from social media:

- You still want to develop your LinkedIn profile & company page. LinkedIn is a powerful place for professionals to share their thought leadership and insights.

- As far as other social channels, it depends on where your audience is; create a company Facebook page, and maybe a Twitter account.

- In Judy's case, we developed the same visuals, high level bio, and other headlines for approval; once approved we uploaded the same bio across all channels.

- We developed a content strategy just to post a few times a week on LinkedIn and Facebook. She has content provided by the company she works with and can leverage then without needing approval.

- We have developed some content from her that we send once a week for review and approval. The down side is that this can make responding quickly a bit challenging.

- We are starting a blog for her.

- Much of the information shared is industry related and news vs. points of view or suggestions which would be against the regulations.

- Judy has won several awards that can also be highlighted once reviewed and approved through compliance.

Blogging is a great way to showcase your capabilities. For example, a law firm might write about questions to ask yourself during estate planning, or contract law. These are high level ways to engage and yet not get into trouble. Many law firms build content around their industry practice to showcase their expertise. There is a "Social Law Firm Index[81]", created by Above the Law and Good2BSocial that assesses practices based on reach, engagement, and owned media. Being social can be done, it just takes planning and an intentional execution of the strategy.

Protecting Your Knowledge, Your Intellectual Property

Dr. Michael Mort, Esq. of Argent Place® Law, PLLC[82], is a lawyer for entrepreneurs and works with them on a myriad of issues — contract law, succession planning, intellectual property, etc. For this section, here are some insights from Dr. Michael Mort that may help you protect the value of your company as well as your own thought leadership. If you write blogs, give presentations, develop your own content, develop products, then you definitely want to read this section. Dr. Mort advocates turning every good idea within your company into intellectual property. There are four main kinds of intellectual property: *Trade Secrets, Trademarks, Copyrights,* and *Patents.* This is not exhaustive, so do talk with your attorney, and this list should at least be helpful.

- *A Trade Secret* can be anything that is not known outside your company, but because you know it you have an advantage over your competitors. Trade Secrets are a form of Intellectual Property, so if you take reasonable steps to protect your secrets, the state and the courts will help you if someone steals them, or tries to.

- *A Trademark* is any "mark" that allows consumers to easily distinguish the maker of one set of goods or services from those of another maker. A trademark can be a word, phrase, symbol, color, sound, design or other device that consumers can rely on to identify the source of certain goods or services. If you register a trademark for a word, phrase, symbol, design or other device in connection with a specific market, you get the exclusive right to use that mark with goods or services in that market and in the jurisdiction where you have registered it. If you register nationally, at the US Patent and Trademark Office, that exclusive right to use extends nationally, and you may attach the famous ® symbol whenever you use your mark.

- Another advantage to registering a trademark is that the law grants favorable remedies to owners of registered trademarks that have been infringed, including legal fees in a civil action to protect your registered mark and hefty damage payments by the infringer, so prospective infringers beware!

Use of the ® symbol puts everyone on notice that you have a registered trademark and you are willing to defend it in the federal courts. But it's against the law to merely attached the ® symbol to your mark without registering it first, so don't take that path. Your trademark attorney can do the work to file your trademark application for you, or you can learn how to do it yourself with the tutorials at www.uspto.gov/trademark.

- You can also use TM or SM if you are claiming common law

- *A Copyright:* Copyright is a body of law that protects authors of creative works. For businesses, those creative works include marketing materials, the content of a website (both words and images), and if you have an interactive website or an app, it includes the code that goes into the website or app.

    - What is important is to know that once you create something, and it is shared publicly, it is in effect copyrighted. You can also add the company name and © copyright with the year and All Rights Reserved. However, just because you do this, it does not prevent someone from copying your work slightly — such as quoting you. However, if you register your works with the Copyright Office, you can defend them, and that allows you to sue someone if they do more than just quote you.

    - Catalog all of your works in your corporate library (digital is easiest)

    - Do consider registering copyright for your blogs, presentations, etc., while taking into consideration there is a processing fee. If you write weekly and share thought leadership, you may want to protect your content by filing monthly or quarterly for a small fee. You may decide to file materials once a year.

- If you have a visual that showcases your thinking and work, you can protect just that page, or entire presentations, again, at your discretion.

- *A Patent:* a patent is for an invention, and is the grant of a property right to the inventor issued by the United States Patent and Trademark Office.[83]

The more content and thought leadership you have, the better positioned your company is to prove its worth and value to potential buyers. Develop an IP strategy with your attorney, especially if you are working to protect your patents internationally in key countries.

Learning to Say No Can Help Protect Your Brand Too

Just as developing your intellectual property is important, which is proactive, there are other ways that a CEO can protect their brand reactively. As a business leader, at any stage of your business, you will always have opportunities that find you. Sometimes these can be distractions, or shiny objects. Other times these opportunities are just what you need to grow. A common challenge is that businesses can stray from their core business and forget what their original mission is, which puts the leadership, employees, customers, and reputation of the company at risk. New Coke is a great example, seemed like a great idea, but we all know how that played out.

ILLUSTRATION
Laura Lee Williams, CEO of Laura Lee Designs, Staying True to the Brand

One evening I hosted an entrepreneur group at my house and was lucky enough to meet Laura Lee Williams, CEO of Laura Lee Designs[84]. She is a gentle force to be reckoned with when it comes to business and growing her business intentionally while taking big risks at the right time in the right way. After studying economics at UCLA and international relations at Harvard, Laura Lee jumped into marketing for companies like Apple, Nike, Ralph Lauren, and American Express. She leveraged her passion for numbers, strategy, and marketing all around world, spending a majority of her time in Hong Kong.

It was while she was in Hong Kong that she had one of those "aha" moments. Standing at the rail station waiting for the next train, she noticed that her silhouette looked just like the woman next to her. In fact, they both had branded handbags, similar clothing, and were almost interchangeable. It is in this moment that Laura Lee began thinking about designing something for a woman that was not about the label, but was about the woman. She sketched her first handbag on a napkin and took it to one of the markets to have a mock up made. When she went back to get her mock up, the seamstress was nowhere to be found. However, Laura Lee continued to go back and about a month later her search paid off as she heard a Chinese woman yelling her name to stop and look at her purse.

The first bag was not great, but Laura Lee kept working at it. She brought the initial pieces home to the United States and soon had family members and friends asking her for them. So in 2004 she had more pieces made and decided to go to New York. Given her focus on creating pieces that were unique and that helped women stand out, she created stunning works of art with over 30,000 beads on each purse, all hand sewn. Due to a conflict of interest with Ralph Lauren, Laura Lee was not able to go to the same sources but she was able to use her resources to land her with a strategic team in Hong Kong, Timbacc International. Due to the paramount quality, she eventually was able to get in front of Henri Bendel and their buyer Foster Chang. As luck would have it, he was of Asian descent and appreciated that her designs were originally launched in China. Chang set up a trunk show right before Christmas and Laura Lee was off and running once she sold two dozen bags. Her focus was to bring her bags into luxury stores like Bloomingdale's, Fred Segal, Ritz Carlton, and more.

The first time Laura Lee was tested was when Macy's asked her to put her bags in their stores. Imagine the distribution and visibility. Laura Lee said no thank you. She knew that this was not the right direction for this luxury handbag, even though most entrepreneurs would have been star struck and said yes. Her biggest concern was that this investment was off brand and would not work out in the long run, only the short run. Her time working with executives in China helped shift how she assessed opportunities and playing the long game.

Laura Lee decided to move production to the United States as a core value, to create jobs in Texas and New York, even though this was a very risky move given her need for high quality while managing costs. It would have been easier to stay in Asia, but to her, this move felt authentic to her brand. Many people, including all of the sharks on Shark Tank, would have said go overseas. To Laura Lee, this was one decision that was the easiest and hardest to make at the time. One of her biggest challenges was finding a manufacturer that could deliver such fine quality, although eventually it worked out.

Laura Lee constantly listens to her customers and looks to create what is meaningful for them. One of the more recent challenges was when she was asked to create bags for sororities. This posed several challenges, getting access to the rights, also what about the Laura Lee Designs luxury brand? Laura Lee made a decision to launch SparkleU[85], another product line separate from her luxury products. This meant creating all new content, social media platforms, marketing materials, and messaging. We developed an entirely different strategy for her social media to intentionally maintain these separate identities.

Many entrepreneurs will face pivots along their journey and will need to true back to their core mission and purpose to ensure investments they make are likely to pay off. For Laura Lee, her mission to create a community around products that build confidence for women, shows up in everything she does from giving back to Breast Cancer events to teaching entrepreneurship at the University of Virginia. In 2006, Eva Longoria carried a Laura Lee handbag during an episode of Desperate Housewives. Then in 2007, Kate Winslet carried one of Laura Lee's handbags at the Academy Awards.

Saying no to investments that take away from the uniqueness of her company is a critical skill that she has leveraged to grow in a tough market — luxury goods. Laura Lee herself is one of a kind and through her bags makes every customer feel that way too.

CHAPTER 8 SUMMARY

Protect Your Brand in Every Interaction

With the advent of the Internet and social media platforms, it may seem that everything is more complicated. Truth be told — it is. That is why it is critical to plan ahead and create reputation management scenarios on a regular basis to prepare for potential issues. Keep your finger on the pulse of your customers, the media, and the public with Google alerts, and other tools like HootSuite[86], SproutSocial, and Simply Measured, to be ready to react quickly and with confidence. Your reputation is all that you have, so manage it as carefully and intentionally as possible.

CHAPTER 9

Build & Deliver on Your CEO Brand Promise In Person & Online

> "It's important to build a personal brand because it's the only thing you're going to have. Your reputation online, and in the new business world is pretty much the game, so you've got to be a good person. You can't hide anything, and more importantly, you've got to be out there at some level."
>
> **GARY VAYNERCHUK**

When you think about building your brand, there are two sides of the same coin: in person and online. As you look at the reputation you are building as the CEO, the critical question is what is the proper blend for in-person versus online interactions, and how do you know what is working? For every CEO, it is important to assess your in person presence as well as your online presence. So far we have discussed in detail a fair amount of in person techniques, like networking and referrals. However, in this chapter we are going to look at how the reputation of the CEO shows up in each day to day decision and interaction — including every online interaction. It will cover understanding why you are online, who needs to see you, what are you actually going to put online, and how to not lose your mind.

The question starts off pretty innocently enough, "where should I be online?" and then the standard answer is usually: once a day on Facebook, five times a day on Twitter, etc. This is not the best advice because it is *so general*. The actual answer should completely depend on where your audience is, how much time you have, what content you are sharing, and what channels makes the most sense. There is no doubt you need to be online; the key questions are:

- Why are you visible?

- Who needs to see what you share?

- What are you sharing?

- When are you sharing it?

Know Why You Are Visible Online and In Person

As the CEO, why are you visible? Earlier, we talked about identifying your critical business goals and putting on paper what your role as the "engaged" CEO should look like for the year ahead. Plan based on the business goals and personal goals to help you decide where you want to stand up and be seen. As the CEO, working with your marketing team, decide which channels you want to be on, what followership you want to have and what that looks like. Is it specifically to engage with employees, clients, media, or all of the above?

For example, in 2014, my goal for visibility as CEO of my own company was 1,000 people. I wanted to see, meet, and talk to 1,000 people. This goal, of course, was part of BrandMirror's overall revenue and social media goals. Then in 2015, my goal ramped up to 10,000 people. This volume was harder and more challenging and demanded that I reach out and set up more speaking engagements and group workshops. There was no way this goal could all be accomplished via one-on-one coaching, however with speaking and workshops, the goal of 10,000 was potentially achievable. For 2016, my goal is to help 100,000 people. However, I know that I do not want to be on a plane traveling every day — so I had to define my tools differently. One of those tools was writing this book. When you think about your visibility goals — what measurable results do you want to see? What crazy goals can you put out there to pressure test your investment decisions and better understand what is scalable and realistic based on the resources you have at this point?

Whether you focus on increasing your visibility online or in person, there are some suggestions that will help you prepare for what to say and share.

Who Needs to See What You Share?

Based on your goals, what people or groups need to see and hear from you online and in person? Earlier we discussed customer segments and why it is very important to examine the demographic and psychographic data to understand who you are talking to online and in person. Here are some tactical suggestions based on where most CEOs engage — if you had to prioritize, start here.

- Update your LinkedIn profile to reflect you and your company (LinkedIn has the most professionals at your fingertips, so for establishing your thought leadership and growing visibility it is a top tool to leverage)

- Choose one or two platforms to use for now (look at the PEW Research on demographics to choose from LinkedIn, Facebook, Twitter, Pinterest, or Instagram, for example), which also align with or augment your company channels

- Identify the channel with the largest following and then invest in the next fastest growing channel or most strategic channel (like Blab or Instagram)

- Choose key content creation goals for your company — for example blog or video blog (vlog) on a regular basis

The above investments will help you start off with the highest touch channels with the goal of increasing awareness, engagement, and giving the company a face.

Optimize Your Online Profiles for Efficiency

As a CEO, solopreneur and founder, you have limited temporal resources. Here are some best practices for integrating your brand with your company on social media and saving time doing so. Individuals can spend anywhere from zero hours to over 40 hours a week. About 60% of CEOs are on social media for one to five hours a week. 43% of CEOs spend more than six hours a week on social media — yikes![87] It depends on your broader strategy, however if you are the only person running the company, these key tips will help you be present and manage your time more effectively.

1. One of the most critical aspects of planning your online strategy is to brainstorm your content. You can develop a host of ideas to work from by thinking and planning ahead.

    a. *Create a library of ideas* that you can pull from on a regular basis.

    b. *Create an editorial calendar* — start with ideas for each month, then each week, then each day

2. Decide which of the top platforms you will use and how you want to show up aligned with the company brand:

    a. *Twitter:* Consider having a company handle @CompanyABC with your name on the profile, CEOName (Example: BrandMirror, Jen Dalton)

b. *LinkedIn:* Do share similar posts on your company page and as well an update on your personal Home page

c. *LinkedIn & Blogging:* re-leverage your blog content on your website and LinkedIn, get the most out of the content you create (be sure to note "Previously seen here" with a link to the original posting site).

d. *Pinterest:* Leverage for sharing pictures and videos, and for creating an "Expert" image, especially for creative or provocative ideas

e. *Instagram:* Leverage images and video to tell a compelling story & engage with your customers

3. *Block your calendar* and pick the amount of time that works for you — even if it is 10 minutes a day or once a week for an hour. If you do not block time, it will not happen.

4. *Identify your top tools* to make your business-life easier. For example, pick a scheduling tool and a content generation tool:

a. *Newsle:* Sign up for this free news analyzer, it communicates with LinkedIn, Facebook, and other channels and alerts[88] you when someone in your network appears in the news (this is a great way to "give, give, get" and invest in your relationships by giving them recognition and celebrating them. Most of us do not like to brag, so if you do it for someone else then that can be a great way to be visible by supporting others). You may want to ask them first, just to be sure it is something they want highlighted.

b. *Get Content Delivered to You:* Choose your topics and then use tools like BuzzSumo, ContentGems, Feedly, and Google Alerts to send you emails everyday (or however you schedule them) which provide articles of special interest to you, etc. This makes it easier to grab and post.

c. *Review Your Scheduled Content Before It Posts:* Although scheduling your content is a great way to go, there are risks to scheduling it. For example, Scott Stratten, the president of Unmarketing, shares this example of really bad timing. Live Nation scheduled a tweet about a Radiohead concert, but unfortunately the concert was canceled due to the stage collapsing and people being injured and one person died. Live Nation tweeted about canceling the show, but 30 minutes later one of their scheduled tweets read "Help us create a @radiohead photo album from the show! Share your Instagram photos from the show tonight with the hashtag #RadioheadTO". You may want to post daily and block 30 minutes a day on your calendar to avoid issues and this allows you to use the most relevant and timely content.

d. *Set up tools to track key words:* For example, with the tool HootsuitePro, you can use #hashtags to follow conversations on Twitter. You can also use Hashtagify[89] to see which hashtags are used the most.

e. *HARO, Help a Reporter Out* — This is a great tool to see what content the media is looking for on a daily basis. With a great pitch and email header, you could get a story featured somewhere exciting!

The below suggestions are guidelines I use for my social media content:

- *The Trifecta:* When you intend to post, think about including these three items to get more visibility: one link, one photo, tag someone. You want to make it easy to engage, tagging someone means you use the @ symbol plus their name to let them know you are mentioning them.

- *Create a Call to Action:* What do you want people to do? Do you want them to sign up for an event, click and sign up for email, like it, retweet it, share it? Be intentional with any post as to why you are doing it and what you want to have happen.

- *Do Not Over #Hashtag:* As a follow on to the above, please do not over #hashtag, it can make you look unprofessional, amateurish, and be a waste of space.

What to Share: The 4 I's That Are Not about You

We often get stuck trying to figure out what to say when we build our brand. It is critical to remember that most of the time your personal brand should not be about you. Here are four key ways to add value and build your thought leadership without talking about yourself and wearing out your welcome. As you build your content strategy for the week, month, and year, this framework can help ensure you deliver on your brand without talking about yourself too much. 90% of the time, or more, you should post content that falls into one of these four buckets.

1. *Inform* When you provide information to your audience, it is a great way to add value. Identify the knowledge you have gained over the years through success or failure. Create little "bundles of knowledge" that you can share.

Examples:

- If you are an entrepreneur, maybe it is about the key information you need to know before you leave your paying job to start your company.

- If you are a lawyer, write about the impacts of new regulation and how it might affect your constituents.

2. *Inspire* Who doesn't want to be inspired? We all need some motivation and inspiration. Do not over post quotes, be thoughtful and intentional about why you are sharing them. Maybe they are related to a time of year or a person — let's say Martin Luther King Jr. — and you want to post it around MLK day.

Recommendations:

- Pictures are more likely to be shared — so turn your quote into a photo and attach it in your Tweet or Facebook post.

- Use tools like Canva to create your image for free.

3. *Influence* For executives and entrepreneurs, it is critical to post content that reflects your thought leadership. This type of content is all about influencing a conversation. What do you believe about an industry or something happening in the world? Think about what you have credibility and permission (from your audience) to talk about that would resonate. You want to break through the noise, not add more noise.

Things to Consider:

- Research what others are saying about the topic and be sure your perspective is not just repeating the same old content.

- Keep it short, sweet, and actionable — make it easy for people to care and share your influential ideas.

4. *Ignite* Spark a conversation. Be thoughtful about being provocative, but not polarizing. Provocative is all about starting a conversation, a dialog.

Things to Consider:

- Be careful of your topic — recommend not talking about religion and politics — unless that is your space (it can be too polarizing)

- Don't be mean. You can ignite a conversation diplomatically; there is no need to ignite a conversation with mean or negative comments. Nothing impacts your credibility more than being mean.

Remember that the purpose of sharing content is to help create value for others. It is not just to hear yourself speak. Share information that is insightful. The odds of it being shared are much greater.

Should I Curate or Create My Content?

When entrepreneurs start on social media, one of the biggest challenges is to identify how much of your content versus someone else's content should be used, especially if you need a lot of content to share across multiple platforms. It is possible that you will want various content every day. So where do you start? For many, the answer is in sourcing the content heavily from experts, or "curating"- then bringing more and more of your own content to bear.

You may start curating 90% of your content and then sharing 10% of your own, or maybe you begin closer to 60% and 40%, curate vs. create. The critical decision here is about the mix, as well as how much total content to include. I gave a talk at Capital One in 2014 and one of the women said she wanted to be visible 12 times a year, which is great, she could blog once a month and be done. I had another woman, who has a photography business, say that she wanted to be visible 5-10 times a month depending on her workload. The most important part of this work is to choose something that you can commit to as well as be involved.

Getting Started is Half the Battle, It Is Never Too Late to Start

It is very important to get started and be consistent. If putting yourself out there is very new, then try doing one thing a month, if you need to do more, then add one thing a week until you get to between three and five actions a week and see how things are going. It is absolutely critical that you listen and pay attention to the pulse of your audience and see what works for them. Every CEO has a reputation already, it is never too late to start defining your reputation intentionally and integrating it into the broader company brand.

A few months ago I attended a speaker series from Her Corner[90] (an entrepreneur network for women) and heard

Jen Bilik, the founder of Knock Knock[91], speak about her experience and lessons learned as an entrepreneur. If you are not familiar with Knock Knock, the company was founded with the mission of creating witty, design-driven gift products and books. These products are in over 6,000 stores nationwide and in 46 countries across the globe. After the talk, I asked if I could interview her to capture where she is at on the personal brand journey in relation to her company. We had a fascinating discussion and she shared her insights into what she plans on next. Knock Knock was founded in 2002 and Jen has been doing regular public speaking since 2006.

In the last few years, however, she has begun to think about her personal brand. In Jen's words, her sense of her personal brand is that it hasn't yet been defined. She started Knock Knock before social media was even around. So now she is working on articulating her brand to support Knock Knock and be a thought leader with respect to her experience as an entrepreneur and a creative person. The biggest gap in her mind is simply thinking through how best to harness who she is and what she has learned as an entrepreneur in a consistent way and with an intentional voice. Jen is absolutely hilarious and is concerned about that getting lost in translation.

Jen has some amazing qualities, and she is absolutely comfortable sharing her vulnerabilities and lessons learned. She has written for Inc.com and the Huffington Post. But felt that those articles, although insightful and true, were not on brand or in her true voice — especially in their lacking humor. If you have a core skill, like humor, or empathy, it's important to leverage that trait throughout your content, in person or online. Jen had the entire group of women entrepreneurs rolling on the floor laughing and also nodding our heads in agreement at the lessons she shared. Her ability to leverage humor intentionally to connect with her audience made her talk more authentic and relevant.

Jen's next opportunity is to build an overall reputation strategy for herself and identify what works for her when it comes to infusing her personality into her insights. She is curious by nature and when you integrate that into her entrepreneurial spirit and knack for comedy, powerful things will happen. Keep in mind that wherever you are, we all had to get started at some point.

CHAPTER 9 SUMMARY

Build & Deliver on Your Promise in Person & Online

Whether you are already on social media, or just getting started, be intentional about how you want to authentically show up. If you don't love writing Tweets or blogging, then step back and look at it again. When you deliver your first talk, or a hundredth talk, are you still enjoying it? Your gut can tell you if what you are sharing online and in person is on point and resonates with you. Don't be afraid to start, ask for help, and go for it. You have something to say, it is worthwhile, and as long as you are writing for the audience and you are authentic, you will succeed. Social media and the internet are here to stay, don't try and be everywhere at once, pick a channel like LinkedIn, and simply start. Be consistent from the beginning, don't start a Twitter account if you are not using it at least once a week. Hence my guidance on start with one, do it well, then expand. It is critical to deliver on what makes you unique in person and online.

"Repetition makes reputation, and reputation makes customers."

ELIZABETH ARDEN

EXERCISE
The 4 Is That Are Not About You

The 4 Is That are Not About You	What could you talk about that is on brand?	Which channels appeal to you and your audience?	What evidence do you need?
Inform			
Influence			
Inspire			
Ignite			

EXERCISE
Curate vs. Create Strategy

Reputation Rings	What content would you need to curate — i.e. find from others?	What content could you create?	What channels work best?

CHAPTER 10

Maintain & Grow Your Impact, Visibility, and Value as a Noisebreaker

> "This is the true joy in life, the being used for a purpose recognized by yourself as a mighty one."
>
> **GEORGE BERNARD SHAW**

As you come to the final chapter of this book, you will get to see examples from outstanding business leaders on how they live their brand. The most critical part of our journey is to be clear on our WHY. Discovering our purpose, why we exist, is the sixty-four million dollar question. For the most part people do not have or know how to take the time to reflect on what they want to contribute and bring to the world. At the beginning of the book, we started focusing on your leadership promise statement. Defining your promise and being clear on what makes you unique is critical to forming the foundation for how you want to make an impact. This concept of being a Noisebreaker implies that you know what the "noise" is, i.e. what the distractions are, and are looking for where you can break through to create value and impact. In this chapter, as in the book, it is important to pull out tangible examples of how everyday people became Noisebreakers. In discovering their WHY, they can cut through the chaos and create meaningful moments for their clients, their teams, their community, their industry, and the world. Each of the following case studies highlights CEOs that have developed a clear WHY and leverage it to grow their business with clarity and confidence.

David Belden: His WHY is to be "A Professional Outsider" for his Clients

I met David Belden in 2014 and instantly knew that he was clear on his purpose, his WHY. One of his favorite quotes is from Leonard Cohen, "...they sentenced me to 20 years of boredom, for trying to change the system from within." For 30 years, David worked in organizations run by other people. He then launched five startups and pulled off three major turnarounds, all successfully, and all fraught with fear and trembling. For the past 17 years, he used that experience in working with over 200 organizations to help them *create cultures where every person is encouraged to contribute at his or her highest level of ability*. Having been inside large, global companies, he had the ability to see their challenges and flaws, and to help his clients avoid making the same mistakes.

When David decided to form ExecuVision International to help companies transform their culture, he needed to differentiate himself from an extremely crowded field. Most people doing this type of work proudly titled themselves "Management" or "Organizational Development" consultants. Since many of them had never actually run companies, David felt that the *con* in *consulting* was ironic.

When potential clients ask him what he does, he discovered that there is one consistent theme in his answer: *his Leadership Promise is to look at organizations and relationships from without to discover elements that cannot be seen from within.* It makes no difference if David is facilitating an executive retreat of senior leaders or executive couples retreat to work on personal relationships. The requirement is the same: to have the skill and the courage to reflect back to people how they show up in any relationship. The objective assessment can only be accomplished by a Professional Outsider.

All of his work has come through referrals though much of the initial interest has come either through public presentations, workshops, internet discussions or blogs. Staying current with a rapidly transforming world, and discovering obscure connections amongst seemingly unrelated events (technological, political, economic, cultural, generational, etc.) are key components of his work. Networking with people who understand complexity and can make sense of the craziness of this historic moment is an underrated investment of time... an investment with incredible returns.

Everyone needs Outsiders. We need them to help us validate what we already sense. The Outsider helps reveal the extent of the challenges and opportunities we face. We help people differentiate what is real and what is a shadow. The Outsider does not offer a solution but instead helps to explore options. The Outsider can see the possibilities; the Insider must take responsibility for choosing the best path forward. David has built his reputation on integrity, and being the professional Outsider. It is even his title on his LinkedIn page. David's WHY shows up in every conversation, every blog, every coaching session. David can also look at his WHY, his Leadership Promise, and assess if he is living up to his promise and identify new innovative ways to deliver on his promise looking ahead.

What metrics and behaviors are needed to deliver on your Leadership Promise?

Dan Berger, Social Tables: When Your WHY Infuses Your Company

A few years ago at a Netcito[92] event (an entrepreneur community), I met fellow Georgetown University Hoya, Dan Berger, who had just come up with this company called Social Tables. Having just completed his MBA at Georgetown in 2010, and while working at Booz Allen Hamilton in 2011, Dan decided to launch Social Tables. It is a hospitality software company that has revolutionized the event planning industry. Social Tables empowers meeting planners from firms of all sizes to make real time room layouts, communicate that vision to their clients, and make seating simple and all online. The software provides a ridiculously fast check-in, and finally — a virtual site for each client to leverage when they are working on sales and marketing. How did Dan get here? Dan describes himself as "scrappy, a hustler, and I never take no for an answer". His focus is on being helpful (sharing and teaching) and connecting people — which clearly shows in the culture and products he has built.

Social Tables has raised nearly $10MM in venture capital and has over 3,500 customers in over 30 countries including Hyatt Hotels, The Venetian-Palazzo, Goldman Sachs, Live Nation, Harvard, and the State Department. Headquartered in DC, the company, and likewise Dan, has won awards in the meeting industry, including the Top 40 Under 40 by Collaborate and Connect Meetings, 2015 Innovator of the Year by Catersource and Event Solutions.

So how did this all happen? When I met Dan, the company was in the idea phase, and he had hired one person to help him get it built and off the ground. He was passionate and relentless in his pursuit of this vision. Early on he knew how important culture was, as well as hiring the right people. In fact, even to this day, he is very engaged in talent management, product development, and enterprise sales.

When looking at your personal brand, it is critical to recognize what you bring to the table that is a special and significant strength. For Dan, it is that he is a people person. He had managed hundreds of people, ran a 15K member association, researched and contributed to an HR book, and is a certified Human Capital Specialist. So when he started his company this idea of being a "people person that builds communities" aligned not only with how he would build his team but it was at the heart of the company he created (and the pain point he was going to solve).

It all started when Dan attended a wedding and did not know anyone at his table. The event seemed like such an opportunity for people to get to know each other, and to make sure guests sat with people that would create the best experience. Eureka! He began to think about how to solve this dilemma. How do you bring people together and make connections possible? Eventually, Social Tables was born. From 2011 to 2015, Dan started with a team of one and had since grown his team and revenue over 100% year over year for three years.

When you look at Dan's brand, here are some key principles that showed up in the beginning when the company started as part of brainstorming sessions with the team:

1. Fail Fast and Often

2. High Risk. High Reward

3. Stop saying ~~No, Because~~ to Yes If...

4. Ship All Day, Party All Night

In Dan's mind, the value of the company and the culture of the company are emblematic of the founding team. In his role as CEO, Dan shared five key lessons he learned at the MAVA[93] (Mid-Atlantic Venture Association) TechBuzz event in 2014 at Georgetown.

1. Get everyone in the same room to talk about the soft stuff such as values, what matters to them, leadership.

2. Iterate as you grow. Continuously learning, for example, even iterating your values as your company grows over time.

3. Align everything in your company to the core values.

4. Craft a shared vision with your team.

5. Align your incentives to your mission and industry.

The vision articulation of the Social Tables values and beliefs show what helps them sleep better at night and keeps them motivated during the day. Below is the latest iteration of the Social Tables culture from the principles highlighted earlier. Dan "believes that every chapter of growth for a company requires revisiting the culture so that it grows with the company". Dan has also written blogs and articles, one of my favorites, The Three Responsibilities of a CEO — Vision, People, and Customers[94]. Dan is committed to laying out a vision, evangelizing it, and removing obstacles in front of it for his team. He pulls in the best talent possible and retains them while scaling a great culture. Lastly, Dan is focused on meeting his customers as much as possible. He described his team like this: "I love my co-workers. They are awesome. Everybody here comes and does what they do in a way that transcends the standard 9-5 job and in a way that connects them to this community and beyond. Work can matter, and it is not just about work, but about building relationships and connections."

Dan believes in creating and inspiring face-to-face experiences through collaboration. The company vision: *We envision a world where people come together to achieve great things.* His core beliefs and values show up in his culture every single day. Even when you go to the Social Tables website[95], Dan's photo is mixed in with everyone else's photo, because they are a team. As far as being social online, Dan is active on Twitter, Facebook, and LinkedIn. Dan is a forward thinker and is proactive in how Social Tables develops thought leadership and shares content as an industry leader.

Latest Social Tables Principles & Values

Recently Social Tables produced a white paper focused on what the event industry would look like 15 years from now. The company continues to define and build its brand day to day in every interaction, with Dan as the visible leader living the brand. Between Dan, his leadership team, and the overall team, they have won over 50 awards, including the Washington Post Best Place to Work, and the Best Culture Award from SmartCEO. Dan started with his vision of building communities and embedded it in his company from day one.

How do you want your beliefs and values to show up in your company?

Gordon Bernhardt, Bernhardt Wealth Management: Celebrating Leaders

In 2015, I was thrilled to get the chance to work with Gordon Bernhardt, the founder and President of Bernhardt Wealth Management. He is a nationally recognized wealth manager, winning the 2015 SmartCEO Money Manager Award. I met him as a Vistage speaker when I gave a talk on creating a CEO and Executive Presence Online, and then we worked together on launching an event for CEOs in the DC market. When I researched his personal brand and delved into his history and background, I was unbelievably impressed with this dedication to living his WHY and supporting those leaders in the community that operate with Character, Chemistry, and Caring. Gordon lives by these same values in his firm: "I established my wealth management firm because I wanted a company that put clients first" said Bernhardt. "We take our fiduciary responsibility — to act solely in our client's best interests — very seriously."[96]

At that point in 2015 Gordon had interviewed over 400 CEOs in the area with significant revenue and growth. His focus was on highlighting others by creating "Profiles in Success." Gordon designed this program to inspire current and future small-business owners with these profiles that provided very personal stories of each CEO and their wisdom gained along the way. The Profiles in Success is an investment in celebrating leaders who are ethical and exhibit behaviors that, in Gordon's mind, is "a much-needed venue" to share with others. So far, Gordon has written 10 volumes and is currently interviewing for volume 11. The interviews and book are all done at no cost to the interviewee; Gordon interviews the CEO, records it, writes up the profile, sends it for review, and then publishes the profile in the next volume.

This special project is separate from Gordon's business[97], which is wealth management. However, it gets him visibility to individuals that could be clients and, more importantly, Profiles in Success reinforces Gordon's reputation as someone who values ethics, character, and leadership. Over the years, Gordon has added in a Profiles in Success Award that is given out each year to peer-nominated leaders from the interviewees. This year it was held at the Ritz Carlton, with close to two hundred leaders in attendance from the DC area.

I chose to highlight this case because Gordon has brilliantly created a program that celebrates individuals, at the same time reinforcing his values, and generates powerful leadership insights for the broader community. As an entrepreneur, creating a program that aligns with your business and values is an intentional way to stay relevant and authentic. You do not have to be at the helm of a large Fortune 500 firm to develop programs that align with your personal beliefs and your company values, all that is required is clarity on the WHY and commitment.

What program could you launch that reflects your reputation and values?

Authors of Relevance: From Writing It to Living It — Relevance, Matter More Meals

Earlier in this book, I wrote about Relevance: Matter More[98], authored by Tom Hayes, Marian Deegan, and Phil Styrlund. Relevance was inspired by the belief that people are all companions on the journey to mattering more. Following the book's launch in the fall of 2014, Tom and Marian began meeting informally with thought leaders in the Twin Cities who were intrigued with possibilities for using the Relevance formula to build a stronger community. Riley Hayes has a reputation for lavish hospitality, fed by Tom Hayes' considerable skills in the kitchen and at the grill—and by the warmth of his Director of Goodwill and Hospitality, Perri Sigfrid (who makes a killer popover)—so these conversations took place over dinners hosted on the Riley Hayes deck, with the glittering Minneapolis skyline as a backdrop. The ideas sparked over Tom's feasts were so inspiring that they decided to make these intimate gatherings a regular event, and founded the Matter More Meals.

Several times a year, they invite a select group of leaders to join them for a Matter More Meal at Riley Hayes. Their guests are respected professionals who contribute perspectives from fields encompassing health care, law, finance, media, education, the creative arts, and the nonprofit world. They choose guests for their commitment to making a difference in their personal lives, in their professional work, and in their communities.

They are proud of the friendships that have been forged during these gatherings, and of the opportunities that have been created through the collaborative discussions and thoughtful reflection fed by good food and great company. Marian shared how they have been honored and delighted by the dynamics put in motion as a result of these evenings:

- Two of their guests have been nominated and recognized as leaders in the Twin Cities health care community.

- An inspiring entrepreneur-nonprofit partnership has been publicly lauded.

- New business relationships were forged.

- Introductions have been made by their guests to connect Marian and Tom to other inspiring leaders in our community.

In 2016, Marian and Tom look forward to continuing the relevance conversations, and sharing quarterly Matter More Meals with like-minded people. On the What's Relevant[99] page of their website, they will be introducing their guests so that anyone can learn with them about these individuals who are dedicated to serving their communities in a variety of inspiring ways that truly matter. They hope that their conversation will generate ideas that help all of them matter more to each other and for each other.

What can you do to be more relevant in your community?

Rachael Watson Every Child Fed: Her WHY Can Be Heard Around the World

In 2013, I learned about Every Child Fed[100], a non-profit focused on ending childhood deaths related to malnutrition through sustainable, empowering and environmentally responsible methods in Zambia. The company held a fantastic New Year's Eve Gala with hundreds of people and members of the Redskins Team, like Kedric Golston, who is on the Every Child Fed Board. It was in 2014 when Rachael and I sat down to work on her personal brand and her story. We met at a coffee shop and began to talk about Every Child Fed and what was next for the organization.

Around the same time Rachael and I sat down in September of 2014, there was a new program, the Presidential Leadership Scholars[101] that launched to increase social good in communities large and small through leadership development. I learned about the program from Paul Almeida[102], the senior associate dean for executive education at the McDonough School of Business at Georgetown University. Professor Almeida and Professor Michael O'Leary from Georgetown are co-leading academic advisors for the program. What is unique about this program is that it draws upon the resources of four presidential centers and foundations, George W. Bush, William J. Clinton, George H.W. Bush, and Lyndon B. Johnson, to train the next generation of bi-partisan leaders. This program is for executives that wanted to lead better and drive social good, while learning from former presidents, key administration officials, and leading academics.

I brought this opportunity to Rachael, and we began to prepare for applying. You know that moment when you realize you need an updated resume and that last time you touched it was years ago? Yes, she had that moment. Rachael and I worked through her story, her why, and leveraged the I.M.P.R.E.S.S. Model ™ to build her resume and overhaul her LinkedIn profile. She worked through the broader application, and we developed her project for the submission. In short order, Rachael was accepted into PLS and joined the inaugural group of sixty leaders. The implications of this were huge: six months of working with leaders from around the country, all committed to driving social good and impact. Rachael shared her experiences with me about speaking with Condoleezza Rice, sitting with former President Bill Clinton at dinner, and working with outstanding thinkers to pressure test her project and how to ensure her initiative was set up to move forward and drive change.

Since we updated her LinkedIn, she has had many people reach out to her for insight, consulting opportunities and partnership offers. However, that is not the most powerful thing Rachael took away from our work together. The most powerful thing was true clarity on her WHY, her ability to articulate her purpose. As an entrepreneur, there is not a day that goes by where we do not face challenges, hard questions, and hard decisions. I always think we have Freedom but no Free Time. In those moments where Rachael was facing an uphill battle to raise more money, pull people together in Zambia from different organizations: her WHY has sustained her and made her focus on what was in her control instead of the obstacles facing her.

Rachael described when she went to the first PLS event and met unbelievable individuals who all seemed more qualified than her to be there. Most of us have been there at some point, you walk into a room and wonder what in the heck you are doing there. We all have to start somewhere. However, the imposter syndrome can strike at any point. At first, when Rachael met me, she thought I would help her with her image, but in reality, a personal brand is much deeper and bigger than that. We worked on how she saw herself and how others perceived her. When Rachael is true to herself and authentic, then she can show up in any room and have the clarity and confidence to be present. Our work helped her be cohesive and consistent with her story and helped her feel more comfortable about how she wanted to make an impact and how to drive Every Child Fed forward.

As a result of the Presidential Leadership Scholars program, Rachael has attended events globally. Most recently, she attended the Clinton Global Initiative alongside prime ministers, business leaders like Bill Gates, and other leaders committed to change. One of the reasons Rachael knew to apply to PLS was because she was deliberate in which opportunities to pursue. She did not have to apply, yet she did. When Rachael was at the Clinton Global Initiative, she went in thinking "I am here to learn and make a difference," no matter who else is in the room, she was confident in her why, her reason to be there. As an entrepreneur, you can stand in the company of others and learn from them, connect with them with intention and credibility, provided you know your WHY (and fend off imposter syndrome).

For Rachael, the next challenge is to continue to support Zambia. She has created partnerships that have helped over 30,000 children go from malnourished and close to death, to surviving and having a future. The factories they have built to create the peanut nutrient solution have created jobs and become a sustainable part of the solution. The more you dig into problems, the bigger they can be, but with clarity on your WHY, you are much more likely to see the end game and move around the obstacles instead of being defeated by them. In Rachael's mind, not being intimidated by the size of an obstacle allows you to focus on moving ahead and not simply stopping. More people could focus on what they can do if they had more clarity on their WHY, and not the obstacles. One would think that hunger should not be an issue in today's world, and yet, it is. Knowing your why allows you not to think of the problem as so big as to not do anything. Your WHY allows you to think about how you can commit in powerful and intentional ways, like Rachael.

Having clarity on your WHY enables you to be gutsy and take more chances on creating opportunities — like applying for the Presidential Leadership Scholars program.

What opportunity do you want to go for that will position you to deliver impact?

Kristina Bouweiri: CEO of Reston Limousine Focuses on Innovation

I met Kristina years ago at the Virginia Women's Business Conference, which she helped found. Since then, it is almost impossible to drive around the DC metro area without seeing a limousine or bus that belongs to the Reston Limousine fleet. Since the 1990s, Kristina has grown Reston Limousine[103] to be the 12th largest limousine service in the United States by focusing the business on delivering consistently on its core values of customer service, safety, diversity, integrity, and being employee centered — while driving innovative programs, award winning marketing campaigns, and creating "long-lasting, prosperous relationships with client partners to help them achieve their goals."

Kristina is very humble; when I asked her about her personal brand she simply said that she is here "to be helpful and useful." She sees herself as the ambassador of Reston Limousine and that her role is to network, grow the business through constant innovation, and give back to the community. She is a member of 10 Boards, 7 Chambers, and always provides products and services for any community organization that approaches the company. She is always available and present to help in whatever way that she can, while always keeping an eye out for new business opportunities.

It was Kristina's focus on listening to her clients that prompted her to diversify into wedding transportation in the 1990s, and then again into government contracts and charter services shortly after that. Knowing that the fleet needs to be moving 24/7, Kristina launched an innovative wine and beer tour that has had a very positive impact to the business while being great for visibility. To increase awareness and engagement, Kristina sends coupons and freebies to the Chambers and non-profits on a regular basis to stay top of mind. She has donated over $1 million in services and products to organizations in her community.

Starting in 2009, Kristina established an innovative Client Appreciation Lunch where she brought together clients in her contact list for a lovely lunch where they could network and be celebrated. Kristina would kick off the meeting with a small speech, a thank you, and then she asked local businesses that were interested in getting in front of her clients to attend and introduce themselves for one minute. This appreciation event grew her business by 27% alone, plus generated enormous business for local entrepreneurs.

As a creator and innovator, Kristina launched Sterling Women in 2008. It is a monthly event where women in business come to learn about other women in business, network, and listen to a great speaker. Since 2008, she is on track to have multiple Sterling Women groups throughout the DC market and nationally.

Kristina is a very intentional person, always connecting and creating value, even in the industry she is in, where help is not usually offered. One of the standout, innovative programs Kristina launched was their RLS Management

Services. This global program is unique in that they have drivers, owners, managers, from all over the world come to the Reston Limousine offices for operator training, Department of Transportation training, driver training, and even training on how to write proposals. It is no surprise that Reston Limousine has been recognized nationally in the industry as Operator of the Year winner numerous times.

Kristina has been recognized as a Power 100 recipient from the Washington Business Journal, a Future 50 by SmartCEO, one of the 5000 Fastest Growing Companies in the United States by Inc., to name a few. With their amazing marketing programs, Reston Limousine received the US Search Award for Best Use of Search and the Landy award for Best overall SEO Initiative by Go Fish Digital.

Kristina constantly invests in her learning and seeks out opportunities to grow. As a member of Vistage, Kristina surrounds herself with other senior business leaders in various industries that provide feedback and insights. She actively participates in the Economic Club of Greater Washington, and is a member of this year's Leadership Greater Washington. She has always been one to focus on "finding blue oceans" and challenging the status quo approach. One of the few females in a male dominated industry, Kristina believes that a business owner should never get comfortable, and that you should always be curious and create the opportunities and solutions you need, don't wait for others to do it for you.

As a thought leader, how are you constantly asking what's next?

Kathy Albarado: Chief Engagement Officer at Helios HR Realizing the Potential in People

When I think about a company that is grounded in the values and purpose of their leader, Kathy Albarado, the Chief Engagement Officer at Helios HR comes to mind instantly. Helios HR is a "relationship company" that happens to specialize in helping companies be more competitive when it comes to attracting, engaging, and retaining talent. What is impressive about Kathy is that she is has built her identity around being "intentional, energetic, authentic, and creating impact" for her employees, network, and industry. Kathy has blended her beliefs and values into the brand of Helios. Here are some excellent examples to see how detailed and intentional Kathy and her team of amazing people are at living their brand.

- Kathy has a reputation for being unbelievably energetic. The logo of her firm and them name align with this. With the rising sun embedded in the name, Helios, which represents the Greek personification of the sun, is all about energy

HELIΩS HR℠

- The color orange, which reflects energy and happiness is woven into everything

- Employees receive an "Orange Allowance" when they join to add to their orange wardrobe, which they wear at Helios events and functions

- Kathy sends out her e-letter titled," On the Horizon", which communicates big goals, opportunities, and more to the team

- With a team of 30 people, and growing, each person gets one on one coaching on a weekly or bi-weekly basis. The focus of Kathy and her leadership team is on developing their people to make a powerful impact and achieve their potential.

- Helios HR does webinars on a regular basis on HR related topics, intentionally providing value and evidence of their insights and expertise

- All of their employees blog on their relative areas of expertise

- Kathy has created a team of brand ambassadors that embody the values of the company. Her clients constantly are amazed at how each employee lives the Helios brand.

- Lastly, Helios HR puts on the Apollo Awards annually, 2016 is their 10th anniversary, to recognize companies with outstanding people practices. The event is at 7:30 in the morning (along with the rising sun) and involves music, orange maracas, and so much energy, it is unbelievable. In fact, you can hear Kathy claim that the Apollo Awards is guaranteed to be the MOST high energy event you will have attended at 7:30 in the morning. To date, no one has challenged that title.

One of the biggest takeaways from Kathy is that Helios articulates their expectations when it comes to values and cultural alignment throughout their recruiting process. Kathy believes that it is their values that are central to the brand, and although many leaders state their values, they do not discuss how the values show up in *behaviors* that bring those values to life. For example, one of the core Helios values is "Being Engaged", as a team, they sit down and share what that means for each of them. Then as team members are engaged, they get shout outs on Yammer (an internal communication tool) to recognize how they demonstrated those values with clients, with each other, and in the community. Helios also recognizes those behaviors at monthly All Hands meetings as well.

Kathy has built a company that is consistently exhibiting and living their values and while being an energizing force for her team, clients, community, and the HR industry. Helios HR was recently awarded the SmartCEO Culture Awards Winner in 2015, along with multiple awards for Corporate Citizenship. Helios HR promises to "make big things happen" through "caring," "intention", and "engagement". Kathy is a "Noisebreaker" and has built a reputation that generates an incredible impact for anyone that interacts with her and Helios HR.

How are you weaving in your brand intentionally through your business?

EXERCISE
Becoming an Intentional Leader

Becoming a Noisebreaker	Where can you break through the noise?
What metrics and behaviors are needed to deliver on your Leadership Promise?	
How do you want your beliefs and values to show up in your company?	
What program could you launch that reflects your reputation and values?	
What can you do to be more relevant in your community?	
What opportunity do you want to go for that will position you to deliver impact?	
As a thought leader, how are you constantly asking what's next?	
How will you leveraging your brand to be a Noisebreaker?	

CHAPTER 10 SUMMARY

How Are You Leveraging Your Brand to be a Noisebreaker?

It is important to be intentional about who you are when it comes to your reputation and values. What do you want to be known for in person, online, and in every interaction? Remember, your personal brand is there for life — a lifetime commitment — which means you want to invest time to get it right. Your personal brand is about you, not just your identity for this company, but defining an overall brand that will last over time and make sense whether you are at this company, a well-known speaker, a CEO at a future business, etc. Your personal brand is meant to be sustainable. You want to understand what you want to be known for and what your leadership promise is over time, not just at this one moment. All of the leaders highlighted in this book showcase clarity on their why, a passion for their work, and build their brand very intentionally.

Be an Intentional Entrepreneur. Be a Noisebreaker, not a Noisemaker.

ACKNOWLEDGEMENTS

This book has been an important growth opportunity for me. When I speak on personal branding, I often talk about identifying your superpower, one word to capture your reputation. My word is *gutsy*. Writing this book and putting my authentic self out there is definitely my attempt at living my brand and sharing frameworks and tools that have worked for me as well as my clients.

A huge thank you to my family, Jerrod, Wyatt, Logan, and my parents, David and Carol, for inspiring me to be my best self and supporting me through this process over the last few months. With lots of late nights and working over the weekends, it has been extremely meaningful to have their support.

One of the chapters in this book talks a lot about building meaningful networks — here are the groups of amazing people that help me learn and want to be better every day.

- Georgetown University McDonough School of Business Executive Coaching Team (Patricia Buchek, Elizabeth (Libby) Graves, and Sandra Buteau). Thank you to Sandra for reading the draft book and providing great feedback.

- My weekly BNI group, Business Networking International, where I have met such amazing people and made friends, who also happen to be outstanding business leaders. A special shout out to Michael Mort and Mark Watson for being in the book. Thank you many of the entrepreneurs in this group who have helped me learn, grow, and be better.

- Georgetown University Women's Leadership Institute with Dr. Cathy Tinsley, Marcia Mintz, and Nicole Ratelle.

- George Mason University Women in Business Initiative comprised of 30 outstanding business leaders in the DC Metro Market. A special thank you to this group of leaders investing in the students, community, and each other to make a difference.

- The Reston Chamber of Commerce has been an outstanding partner in the community and introduced me to wonderful business owners — their programming is great and I look forward to working with them more.

- The Loudoun Chamber of Commerce has also been a great partner with their wonderful network and Small Business Awards that recognize wonderful companies each year.

- Last, but not least, Her Corner, led by Fred Campagne Irwin, where I have met outstanding women entrepreneurs, amazing speakers, and learned more about my business, myself, and grown tremendously over the last three years.

I cannot say enough how important it is to have a diverse network that builds deep relationships.

To each of the entrepreneurs I highlight in the book, thank you so much for allowing me to include you and feature you as Intentional Entrepreneurs.

- Nanette Parsons, Best Rack Around in Leesburg, VA

- Donna Hoffman, Women on Course

- Marian Deegan, Tom Hayes, authors of *Relevance: Matter More*

- Jen Bilik, founder of Knock Knock

- Maura Fredericks, founder of Thrive Consulting & Coaching, LLC

- Jamie McIntyre, founder of Rewire

- Jo Ann Skinner, founder of Opening Doors to Growth

- Kathy Albarado, founder of Helios HR

- Judy Redpath, founder of VISTA Wealth Strategies, LLC

- Mark Watson, co-founder of Exterior Medics

- Dr. Michael Mort, Esq. of Argent Place® Law, PLLC

- David Belden, founder of ExecuVision

- Dan Berger, founder of Social Tables

- Gordon Bernhardt, founder of Bernhardt Wealth Management

- Rachael Watson, CEO of Every Child Fed

- Francisca Alonso, co-founder of AV Architects + Builders

- Jill Erber, Owner of Cheesetique

- Kristina Bouweiri, CEO of Reston Limousine, Founder of Sterling Women

- Laura Lee Williams, CEO of Laura Lee Designs

- Cyndy Porter, Cyndy Porter Style & Photography

Thank you to the dozens of advance readers, I really appreciate your input, investment, and generosity.

A special thanks to friends and business owners who read this before it was even ready to go to others:

- Shye Gilad, founder of ProJet, Business Owner's Radio, and Creating Lift

- Talmar Anderson, founder of Talmar It Up, LLC

- Raad Alkadiri, Managing Director at IHS

- Lisa Katzman, my Marketing & Branding associate

- Michael Cheung, SVP, Credit and Operations at FastPay

- Sandra Buteau, member of the Executive Coaching team at Georgetown University

A huge thank you goes out to Professor Jeanine Turner of Georgetown University, who wrote the Foreword to the book and has been such a great friend, sounding board, and outstanding teacher when it comes to communication for executives and helping them have a great impact through better, more intentional communication. Her class was absolutely one of the most important I ever took as an Executive MBA student.

Thank you The Difference Press, Angela Laurie, Mila, and Kelly for providing a great process to launch a book. It was much easier to get my thoughts on paper with them on my team.

Thank you again to all of you for making this possible. A special shout out to thought leaders that have inspired me. William Arruda, founder of REACH, and Seth Godin, author of so many of my favorite books. What is amazing about Seth Godin and William Arruda, is that I emailed them both about the book and they both got back to me within the hour. Thank you both for being an inspiration to me and playing an important role in bringing this book to life.

ABOUT THE AUTHOR

Jen Dalton, CEO of BrandMirror, has over 15 years of experience in strategy, marketing and coaching. In 2012, after graduating from the Georgetown University Executive MBA program, she made a gutsy move and launched her branding business. Jen has since become a REACH certified master personal branding strategist.

Some of Jen's first clients were her classmates, individuals who realized if they wanted to get to the next level, then investing in their brand was the most effective way to do that. Since then, Jen has worked with individuals, teams, and CEOs to more clearly articulate their stories, value, and their leadership promise to take their businesses to the next level.

Jen specializes in working with CEOs on defining their thought leadership on LinkedIn and other social media. She has spoken to and coached thousands of individuals and entrepreneurs on how to define their brands, craft their stories, stand out, and be relevant. She is an international speaker and has worked with the Navy, GE, IBM, Capital One, UXPA, 1776, C-Lever, and more.

Jen joined the Executive Coaching team at Georgetown University in 2014 and works with their Executive MBA candidates. She is a Senior Industry Fellow at the Georgetown University Women's Leadership Institute, supporting their branding and marketing efforts around gender equity and leadership. Jen believes you need to be a noisebreaker, not a noise-maker. She is a mom to two boys, wife to a husband who is as introverted as she is extroverted. She loves singing, dancing, and laughing.

THANK YOU!

Thank You & Access Your Bonus Materials!

To say thank you and help you succeed as an Intentional Entrepreneur, we have created a workbook of the exercises and uploaded it to www.brandmirror.com.

You will be able to access the Worksheets and Tools page (the password is noisebreaker), which will provide the following resources:

- The Intentional Entrepreneur workbook

- *The Bonus Chapter: 10 Insights for Generating Business on LinkedIn*

- List of Tools mentioned in the book, which we will add to and update as we learn new things

Send me your ideas or questions at: getgoing@brandmirror.com.

Also, follow me on:

Twitter @BrandMirror, Facebook: BrandMirror, YouTube: BrandMirror, and connect with me on LinkedIn, too.

Join our Noisebreaker group on LinkedIn and on Facebook.

Be your best self,
Jen Dalton

ENDNOTES

1 "Delivering Happiness", accessed January 2, 2016. Tony Hsieh's first book, Delivering Happiness, A Path to Profits, Passion, and Purpose. http://delivering-happiness.com/ Companies with a higher sense of purpose outperform others by 400%

2 Jacquelyn Smith, Forbes Staff. October 5th, 2012. "Steve Jobs Always Dressed Exactly the Same. Here's Who Else Does."

http://www.forbes.com/sites/jacquelynsmith/2012/10/05/steve-jobs-always-dressed-exactly-the-same-heres-who-else-does/

3 The Guardian.com. Source: Reuters. Video "Mark Zuckerberg stuns Beijing crowd by speaking Mandarin." Thursday, October 23rd, 2014.

http://www.theguardian.com/technology/video/2014/oct/23/mark-zuckerberg-beijing-speaks-mandarin-video

4 Weber Shandwick | KRC Research. The Social CEO: Executives Tell All PDF. Accessed January 2, 2016.

https://www.webershandwick.com/uploads/news/files/Social-CEO-Study.pdf

5 Weber Shandwick | KRC Research. The Social CEO: Executives Tell All PDF. Accessed January 2, 2016. https://www.webershandwick.com/uploads/news/files/Social-CEO-Study.pdf Weber Shandwick // The Social CEO: Executives Tell All// page 4

6 Cavan Sieczkowski, "Chick-Fil-A CEO Dan Cathy Speaks Out on Gay Marriage." The Huffington Post. March 17th, 2014. Accessed on January 2, 2016.

http://www.huffingtonpost.com/2014/03/17/chick-fil-a-dan-cathy-gay-mar-riage_n_4980682.html

7 Cavan Sieczkowski, "Chick-Fil-A CEO Dan Cathy Speaks Out on Gay Marriage." The Huffington Post. March 17th, 2014. Accessed on January 2, 2016.

http://www.huffingtonpost.com/2014/03/17/chick-fil-a-dan-cathy-gay-marriage_n_4980682.html

8 Cavan Sieczkowski, "Chick-Fil-A CEO Dan Cathy Speaks Out on Gay Marriage." The Huffington Post. March 17th, 2014. Accessed on January 2, 2016.

http://www.huffingtonpost.com/2014/03/17/chick-fil-a-dan-cathy-gay-marriage_n_4980682.html

9 Weber Shandwick | KRC Research. The Social CEO: Executives Tell All PDF. Accessed January 2, 2016.

https://www.webershandwick.com/uploads/news/files/Social-CEO-Study.pdf

10 Deepa Prahalad , "Why Trust Matters More Than Ever for Brands." Harvard Business Review. Accessed on January 2, 2016.

https://hbr.org/2011/12/why-trust-matters-more-than-ev/

11 Brandstand — taking a position, putting your stake in the ground, taking a stand as a leader.

12 "CEO Reputation Greatly Impacts Consumer Images of Companies, Weber Shandwick Survey Finds. PR Newswire. May 2nd, 2012. Accessed on January 2nd, 2016.

http://www.prnewswire.com/news-releases/ceo-reputation-greatly-impacts-consumer-images-of-companies-weber-shandwick-survey-finds-149818755.html

13 Andrea Lucas, "Loudoun Small Business Awards — Finalists." September 21st, 2015. Accessed January 2, 2016.

http://www.loudounchamber.org/chamberinsider/2015-Small-Business-Awards-Finalists

14 Visit their store online. Best Rack Around. Accessed on January 2, 2016.

http://www.bestrackaround.com/

15 Donna Hoffman on LinkedIn

https://www.linkedin.com/in/donnahoffmanwomenoncourse

16 Naming Tool & Social Media Availability Tool: Knowem. Accessed on January 2, 2016.

http://knowem.com/

17 SBA U.S. Small Business Administration ,"Choose Your Business Name." SBA Naming Suggestions & Tips. Accessed on January 2, 2016.

https://www.sba.gov/content/how-name-business

18 USPTO Search Website & Tool

http://www.uspto.gov/trademarks-application-process/search-trademark-database

19 Mark Lasswell , "Lost in Translation Time and again, product names in foreign lands have come back to haunt even the most brilliant of marketers." CNN Money. August 1ˢᵗ, 2004. Accessed on January 2, 2016.

http://money.cnn.com/magazines/business2/business2_archive/2004/08/01/377394/

20 "Threshold Counsel PC" Visit the website to learn more about legal counsel options for small business owners.

http://threshold.cc/

21 360°Reach is the first and leading web-based personal brand assessment that helps you get the real story about how you are perceived by those around you.

http://www.reachcc.com/360reach

22 "StrengthsFinder". Tool to help identify your strengths. Accessed on January 2, 2016.

http://www.strengthsfinder.com/home.aspx

23 Marcus Buckingham, Read more about the "Now, Discover Your Strengths." Amazon. Accessed January 2, 2016.

http://www.amazon.com/Discover-Your-Strengths-Marcus-Buckingham/dp/0743518144

24 William Arruda, "William's Words: Personal Branding Works.". Reach Personal Branding. June 28ᵗʰ, 2012. Accessed on January 2, 2016.

http://www.reachpersonalbranding.com/2012/06/

25 Phil Styrlund. Tom Hayes. Marian Deegan. "Relevance: Matter More." Amazon. Accessed on January 2, 2016.

http://www.amazon.com/Relevance-Matter-More-Phil-Styrlund/dp/0996018301

26 Phil Styrlund, "Relevance...Mattering More to Others...For Others: Phil Styrlund at TEDxRockCreekPark." TEDx Video accessed on January 2, 2016.

https://www.youtube.com/watch?v=K1a11Y-ynOE

27 "Women on Course." Accessed on January 2, 2016.

https://www.womenoncourse.com/

28 Nick Craig and Scott A. Snook. "From Purpose to Impact". Harvard Business Review. May 2004 Issue. Read the Harvard Business Review article here.

https://hbr.org/2014/05/from-purpose-to-impact

29 "Quora." Visit the website to search for answers and post questions and answers. Accessed on January 2, 2016.

https://www.quora.com/

30 "LinkedIn." Accessed on January 2, 2016.

www.LinkedIn.com

31 "Yelp."

www.yelp.com

32 "Pinterest."

https://www.pinterest.com/

33 "Instagram"

http://www.instagram.com/

34 "Youtube"

https://www.youtube.com/

35 Maeve Duggan, "The Demographics of Social Media Users". PEW Research Center. Internet, Science & Tech. August 19th, 2015. Accessed on January 2, 2016.

http://www.pewinternet.org/2015/08/19/the-demographics-of-social-media-users/

36 Ken Dooley, "How to Over Come the 'Status Quo' of Customers." Customer Experience Insight. Accessed on January 2, 2016.

http://www.customerexperienceinsight.com/how-to-overcome-the-status-quo-of-customers/

37 "The Physics Classroom."

http://www.physicsclassroom.com/class/newtlaws/Lesson-1/Newton-s-First-Law

38 "Microsoft." "How does digital affect Canadian attention spans?" Accessed on January 2, 2016.

http://advertising.microsoft.com/en/cl/31966/how-does-digital-affect-canadian-attention-spans

39 Kevin McSpadden, "You Now Have a Shorter Attention Span Than a Goldfish." TIME. May 14th, 2015. Accessed on January 2, 2016.

http://time.com/3858309/attention-spans-goldfish/

40 Carol Kinsey Goman, "Seven Seconds to Make a First Impression." Forbes. February 23rd, 2011. Accessed on January 2, 2016.

http://www.forbes.com/sites/carolkinseygoman/2011/02/13/seven-seconds-to-make-a-first-impression/

41 Visit the website of Maura Fredericks.

http://www.maurafredericks.com/

42 Nancy Katz, Harvard University, David Lazer, Harvard University, Holly Arrow, University of Oregon, Noshir Contractor, University of Illinois at Urbana-Champaign. "Network Theory and Small Groups." Harvard University. June 2004. Small Group Research, Vol. 35 No. 3, June 2004 307–322. Accessed PDF on January 2, 2016.

http://www.hks.harvard.edu/davidlazer/files/papers/Lazer_Katz_Small_Group.pdf

43 Nancy Katz, Harvard University, David Lazer, Harvard University, Holly Arrow, University of Oregon, Noshir Contractor, University of Illinois at Urbana-Champaign. "Network Theory and Small Groups." Harvard University. June 2004. Small Group Research, Vol. 35 No. 3, June 2004 307–322. Accessed PDF on January 2, 2016.

http://www.hks.harvard.edu/davidlazer/files/papers/Lazer_Katz_Small_Group.pdf

44 Nancy Katz, Harvard University, David Lazer, Harvard University, Holly Arrow, University of Oregon, Noshir Contractor, University of Illinois at Urbana-Champaign. "Network Theory and Small Groups." Harvard University. June 2004. Small Group Research, Vol. 35 No. 3, June 2004 307–322. Accessed PDF on January 2, 2016.

http://www.hks.harvard.edu/davidlazer/files/papers/Lazer_Katz_Small_Group.pdf

45 Alicia Morga, "What is Homophily?" Fast Company. June 28th, 2011. Accessed on January 2, 2016.

http://www.fastcompany.com/1763558/what-homophily

46 Hot Mommas Project

http://hotmommasproject.org/caseview.aspx?id=701

47 Mehrabian, Albert (1971). Silent Messages (1st ed.). Belmont, CA: Wadsworth. ISBN 0-534-00910-7

48 "UCLA" UCLA Faculty

https://www.psych.ucla.edu/faculty/page/mehrab

49 Gregory Ciotti, "The Psychology of Color in Marketing and Branding", Entrepreneur. Accessed on January 2, 2016.

http://www.entrepreneur.com/article/233843

50 "Marketo". Infographic: True Colors: What your brand colors say about your business?

http://www.columnfivemedia.com/work-items/infographic-true-colors-what-your-brand-colors-say-about-your-business

51 "99Designs"

http://99designs.com/

52 "Fiverr"

https://www.fiverr.com/

53 "InspirationLab" April, 2010. Accessed on January 2, 2016.

https://inspirationlab.files.wordpress.com/2010/04/infographiclarge_v2.png

54 "FontFace.Ninja". Easily identify fonts on a website with this tool.

http://fontface.ninja/

55 Christopher Gimmer, "17 Amazing Sites with Breathtaking Free Stock Photos," Bootstrapbay. August 27th, 2015. Accessed on January 2nd, 2016.

https://bootstrapbay.com/blog/free-stock-photos/

56 "Canva". Provides great social media templates for photos, adding quotes, including your logo, etc.

www.canva.com

57 "Wisestamp." Email Signature Tools.

http://www.wisestamp.com/

58 "Newoldstamp."

https://newoldstamp.com/

59 "Vistaprint"

www.vistaprint.com

60 "MOO"

https://www.moo.com/

61 "HeartstringsApp."A Rewire Application by Jamie McIntyre.

http://www.heartstringsapp.com/

62 Jennifer Dalton, "5 Mistakes You are Making on LinkedIn." LinkedIn. February 8th, 2015. Read the post here:

https://www.linkedin.com/pulse/5-mistakes-you-making-linkedin-jennifer-dalton?trk=mp-reader-card

63 "Opening Doors to Growth." Jo Ann Skinner's company website.

http://www.joannskinner.com/

64 Art Kohn, "Brain Science: The Forgetting Curve — the Dirty Secret of Corporate Training." Learning Solutions Magazine. March 13th, 2014. Read more on learning and retention here:

http://www.learningsolutionsmag.com/articles/1379/brain-science-the-forgetting-curvethe-dirty-secret-of-corporate-training

65 "LinkedIn Slideshare" — where you can upload presentations, pdfs, etc.

http://www.slideshare.net/

66 "Weber Shandwick | KRC Research." The CEO Reputation Premium: Gaining Advantage in the Engagement Era.

http://www.webershandwick.com/uploads/news/files/ceo-reputation-premium-executive-summary.pdf

67 "Exterior Medics." Learn more about this company in the DC Metro area and how they have brought their values into their work and workplace.

http://www.exteriormedics.com/

68 Cheesetique, a specialty cheese and wine business with multiple locations

http://cheesetique.com/

69 "Buffer." Buffer is a social media management tool.

www.bufferapp.com

70 "Fivver." Fiverr is an online freelance resource:

https://www.fiverr.com/

71 FlexJobs is a resource for employers and job seekers to do freelance, part-time, telecommute.

www.flexjobs.com

72 "CorpsTeam." Corps Team is a resource for strategic workforce solutions.

https://www.momcorps.com/

73 Vistage is a CEO and executive peer to peer advisory group globally with over 20,000 members.

www.vistage.com

74 Young Presidents' Organization

http://www.ypo.org/

75 Entrepreneur's Organization

https://www.eonetwork.org/

76 Claire Zillman, "6 Execs Who Bad-Mouthed Their Own Customers." Fortune. November 13th, 2013.

http://fortune.com/2013/11/13/6-execs-who-bad-mouthed-their-own-customers/

77 Office of Public Affairs, National Labor Relations Board, "Acting General Counsel releases report on social media cases." National Labor Relations Board. August 18th, 2011.

https://www.nlrb.gov/news-outreach/news-story/acting-general-counsel-releases-report-social-media-cases

78 Adidas®: adidas® Group Social Media Guidelines

http://blog.adidas-group.com/wp-content/uploads/2011/06/adidas-Group-Social-Media-Guidelines1.pdf

79 HP, "HP Blogging Code of Conduct"

http://www.hp.com/hpinfo/blogs/codeofconduct.html

80 Jennifer Amanda Jones, "10 Tips for Creating a Social Media Policy for your Business." Social Media Examiner. February 9th, 2012.

http://www.socialmediaexaminer.com/10-tips-for-creating-a-social-media-policy-for-your-business/

81 Brian Dalton, "Which firms are most effective with social media?" Above the Law. January 27th, 2015.

http://abovethelaw.com/2015/01/which-firms-are-most-effective-with-social-media/

82 Dr. Michael Mort, Esq., "What You Should Be Working on Right Now, Part 1."Argent Place® Law PLLC

http://www.argentplacelaw.com/2014/12/what-you-should-be-working-on-right-now-part-i/

83 USPTO, "General Information Concerning Patents." United States Patent and Trademark Office. October 2014.

http://www.uspto.gov/patents-getting-started/general-information-concerning-patents#heading-2

84 Laura Lee Williams Design website

http://www.lauraleedesigns.com/

85 Sparkle U website

http://www.lauraleedesigns.com/sparkle-u/

86 "Hootsuite". A social media scheduling, analytics, and reporting tool:

https://hootsuite.com/

87 Neil Patel, "Don't Waste Your Time: 6 Ways to Be More Efficient on Social Media." Quicksprout. August 10th, 2015.

http://www.quicksprout.com/2015/08/10/dont-waste-your-time-6-ways-to-be-more-efficient-on-social-media/

88 "Newsle." This is a great tool, now part of LinkedIn, that tells you when you friends are in the news. This is a great way to give a shout out and be visible without talking about yourself.

https://newsle.com/

89 Hashtagify — a site that allows you to search potential hashtag words to see how often they are used.

http://hashtagify.me/

90 "Her Corner," Her Corner is a community for women business owners who want to collaborate with others in order to grow their businesses.

http://www.hercorner.org/

91 "Knock Knock," independent makers of clever gifts, books, and whatever else they can think up. Their mission is to bring humor, creativity, and smarts to everyday life.

http://knockknockstuff.com/

92 "Netcito", connect with other entrepreneurs and find the inspiration to succeed.

https://netcito.com/

93 "MAVA," MAVA shines the spotlight on the hottest up-and-coming early stage technology companies in the Mid-Atlantic.

http://www.mava.org/

94 Dan Berger, "The Three Responsibilities of a CEO." Medium. October 25th, 2015.

https://medium.com/@danberger/the-three-responsibilities-of-the-ceo-9534f7d428c6

95 "Social Tables," the number one software for planners and properties to work together online.

https://www.socialtables.com/team

96 Bernhardt Wealth Management Press Release, "Gordon Bernhardt Receives 2015 SmartCEO Money Manager Award." NEWS. November 16th, 2015.

http://bernhardtwealth.com/wp-content/uploads/2015/08/SmartCEO_MoneyManagerAward_20151.pdf

97 "Bernhardt Wealth Management. Visit their website.

http://bernhardtwealth.com/

98 Phil Styrlund. Tom Hayes. Marian Deegan. "Relevance: Matter More." Amazon. Accessed on January 2, 2016.

http://www.amazon.com/Relevance-Matter-More-Phil-Styrlund/dp/0996018301

99 "Relevance: Matter More," Visit their website and learn more about the Matter More dinners and how to be relevant.

http://www.relevancemattermore.com/

100 "Every Child Fed," Visit the ECF website and learn about how they make a difference.

http://everychildfed.org/

101 "Presidential Leadership Scholars," Learn more about this leadership program for social impact and global solutions.

http://www.presidentialleadershipscholars.org/

102 Natalia Rankine-Galloway, "Paul Almeida Training Next Gen Bipartisan Leaders." Georgetown University McDonough School of Business. May 14th, 2015.

http://socialenterprise.georgetown.edu/2015/05/training-next-gen-bipartisan-leaders/

103 Reston Limousine

https://www.restonlimo.com/

difference press

Difference Press offers entrepreneurs, including life coaches, healers, consultants, and community leaders, a comprehensive solution to get their books written, published, and promoted. A boutique-style alternative to self-publishing, Difference Press boasts a fair and easy-to-understand profit structure, low-priced author copies, and author-friendly contract terms. Its founder, Dr. Angela Lauria, has been bringing to life the literary ventures of hundreds of authors-in-transformation since 1994.

LET'S MAKE A DIFFERENCE WITH YOUR BOOK
You've seen other people make a difference with a book. Now it's your turn. If you are ready to stop watching and start taking massive action, reach out.

"Yes, I'm ready!"

In a market where hundreds of thousands books are published every year and are never heard from again, all participants of The Author Incubator have bestsellers that are actively changing lives and making a difference.

In two years we've created over 134 bestselling books in a row, 90% from first-time authors. We do this by selecting the highest quality and highest potential applicants for our future programs.

Our program doesn't just teach you how to write a book—our team of coaches, developmental editors, copy editors, art directors, and marketing experts incubate you from book idea to published bestseller, ensuring that the book you create can actually make a difference in the world. Then we give you the training you need to use your book to make the difference you want to make in the world, or to create a business out of serving your readers. If you have life-or world-changing ideas or services, a servant's heart, and the willingness to do what it REALLY takes to make a difference in the world with your book, go to http://theauthorincubator.com/apply/ to complete an application for the program today.

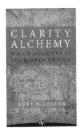

*Clarity Alchemy:
When Success Is
Your Only Option*

by Ann Bolender

*Cracking the Code:
A Practical Guide
to Getting You
Hired*

by Molly Mapes

*Divorce to Divine:
Becoming the
Fabulous Person
You Were Intended
to Be*

by Cynthia Claire

*Facial Shift:
Adjusting to an
Altered Appearance*

by Dawn Shaw

*Finding Clarity:
Design a Business
You Love and
Simplify Your
Marketing*

by Amanda H.
Young

*Flourish: Have
It All Without
Losing Yourself*

by Dr. Rachel Talton

*Marketing
To Serve: The
Entrepreneur's
Guide to Marketing
to Your Ideal
Client and Making
Money with Heart
and Authenticity*

by Cassie Parks

*NEXT: How to
Start a Successful
Business That's
Right for You and
Your Family*

by Caroline Greene

Pain Free: How I Released 43 Years of Chronic Pain

by Dottie DuParcé (Author), John F. Barnes (Foreword)

Secret Bad Girl: A Sexual Trauma Memoir and Resolution Guide

by Rachael Maddox

Skinny: The Teen Girl's Guide to Making Choices, Getting the Thin Body You Want, and Having the Confidence You've Always Dreamed Of

by Melissa Nations

The Aging Boomers: Answers to Critical Questions for You, Your Parents and Loved Ones

by Frank M. Samson

The Incubated Author: 10 Steps to Start a Movement with Your Message

by Angela Lauria

The Intentional Entrepreneur: How to Be a Noisebreaker, Not a Noisemaker

by Jen Dalton (Author), Jeanine Warisse Turner (Foreword)

The Paws Principle: Front Desk Conversion Secrets for the Vet Industry

by Scott Baker

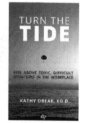

Turn the Tide: Rise Above Toxic, Difficult Situations in the Workplace

by Kathy Obear

Made in the USA
Lexington, KY
04 February 2017